KUNDALINI AWAKENING

A Comprehensive Guide for Beginners to Master the Art and Practice of Kundalini Yoga

NADIA CUNNINGHAM

© **Copyright 2023 by NADIA CUNNINGHAM - All rights reserved.**

This document is geared towards providing exact and reliable information regarding the topic and issue covered. The publication is sold with the idea that the publisher is not required to render accounting, officially permitted, or otherwise, qualified services. If advice is necessary, legal, or professional, a practiced individual in the profession should be ordered.

From a Declaration of Principles which was accepted and approved equally by a Committee of the American Bar Association and a Committee of Publishers and Associations.

In no way is it legal to reproduce, duplicate, or transmit any part of this document in either electronic means or in printed format. Recording of this publication is strictly prohibited and any storage of this document is not allowed unless with written permission from the publisher. All rights reserved.

The information provided herein is stated to be truthful and consistent, in that any liability, in terms of inattention or otherwise, by any usage or abuse of any policies, processes, or directions contained within is the solitary and utter responsibility of the recipient reader. Under no circumstances will any legal responsibility or blame be held against the publisher for any reparation, damages, or monetary loss due to the information herein, either directly or indirectly.

Respective authors own all copyrights not held by the publisher.

The information herein is offered for informational purposes solely and is universal as so. The presentation of the information is without a contract or any guaranteed assurance.

The trademarks used are without any consent, and the publication of the trademark is without permission or backing by the trademark owner. All trademarks and brands within this book are for clarifying purposes only and are the owned by the owners themselves, not affiliated with this document.

Table of Contents

INTRODUCTION 7

CHAPTER 1
THE DIFFERENT TYPES OF YOGA 10
1.1 Yoga 10
1.2 Bikram Yoga 10
1.3 Kundalini Yoga 11
1.4 Hatha Yoga 12
1.5 Vinyasa Yoga 12
1.6 Viniyoga 13
1.7 Ashtanga Yoga 14
1.8 Yin Yoga 14
1.9 Iyengar Yoga 15
1.10 Restorative Yoga 16
1.11 Prenatal Yoga 16
1.12 Power Yoga 17
1.13 Kripalu Yoga 18
1.14 Integral Yoga 18
1.15 Sivananda Yoga 19
1.16 Jivamukti Yoga 19
1.17 Anusara Yoga 20
1.18 Ishtana Yoga 20
1.19 Karma Yoga 21
1.20 Couples Yoga 22
1.21 Laughter Yoga 23
1.22 Acro Yoga 23
1.23 Ananda Yoga 24
1.24 Kriya Yoga 25
1.25 Strala Yoga 25
1.26 Svaroopa Yoga 26

1.27 White Lotus Yoga 27
1.28 Kali Ray Triyoga...27

CHAPTER 2
TYPES OF ENERGY 29
2.1 Kundalini Energy 29
2.2 Dharma 30
2.3 Karma 31
2.4 The Nature of Prana 32

CHAPTER 3
THE FIVE ELEMENTS IN YOGA.. 36
3.1 Fire Element...37
3.2 Water Element...37
3.3 Earth Element... 38
3.4 Ether Element... 38
3.5 Air Element... 38

CHAPTER 4
THE FOUR PATHS OF YOGA... 39
4.1 Bhakti Yoga 39
4.2 Karma Yoga 40
4.3 Raja Yoga 40
4.4 Jnana Yoga 41

CHAPTER 5
THE BASICS OF KUNDALINI YOGA 42
5.1 Five Basic Aspects of Kundalini Yoga.............................. 44
5.2 The Four Body Locks... 46

CHAPTER 6
THE HISTORY OF KUNDALINI YOGA 49

CHAPTER 7
THE CHAKRAS 52
7.1 Muladhara, the Root Chakra..55

7.2 Swadhisthana, the Sacral Chakra 56
7.3 Manipura, the Solar Plexus Chakra 57
7.4 Anahata, the heart chakra 59
7.5 Vishuddha, the Throat Chakra 60
7.6 Ajna, third eye chakra 61
7.7 Sahasrara, the Crown Chakra 62

CHAPTER 8
KUNDALINI AWAKENING 64
8.1 How Safe is Kundalini Awakening? 68
8.2 Signs and Symptoms of Kundalini Awakening 68
8.3 What Can You Do to Experience Kundalini Awakening? . 70

CHAPTER 9
PSYCHIC ABILITY THROUGH YOGA 79
9.1 Ajna Dhyana Meditation 79
9.2 Samyama Meditation 80

CHAPTER 10
POSTURES FOR THE NERVOUS SYSTEM 82
10.1 Balasana 82
10.2 Halasana 83
10.3 Ardha Matsyendrasana 84
10.4 Anuloma Viloma 85
10.5 Adho Mukha Svanasana 85

CHAPTER 11
POSTURES FOR SEXUAL ABILITIES 87
11.1 Reclined Cobbler's Pose 87
11.2 Downward Dog Pose 88
11.3 Cat and Cow Pose 89
11.4 Bridge Pose 90
11.5 11.6. Chair Pose 90

CHAPTER 12
THE HEALTH AND WELLNESS BENEFITS OF YOGA 92
12.1 Why Should We Practice Yoga? 92
12.2 Diabetes 93
12.3 Hypertension 94
12.4 Cholesterol 94
12.5 Mental Health 95
12.6 Skin and Hair 95
12.7 Weight-Loss 96

CHAPTER 13
KUNDALINI MEDITATIONS 97
13.1 The Prayer Pose 98
13.2 Easy Breathing 101
13.3 How to Bring Coordination to Your Body 106
13.4 Meditation for Concentration 108
13.5 Mahan Jaap 111
13.6 Breathing Through Alternate Nostrils 113
13.7 Salabhasana Meditation 115
13.8 Trikonasana Meditation 118
13.9 Savasana Meditation 120
13.10 Three-Stroke Breathing Meditation 121
13.11 Meditation for Happiness 123
13.12 Meditation to Face Tomorrow 126
13.13 Meditation for a Better Future 128
13.14 Kirtan Kriya 131
13.15 Calm Heart Meditation 134
13.16 Meditation for Wisdom 136
13.17 Meditation to Overcome Self Animosity 138
13.18 Meditation to Increase Spiritual Stamina 140
13.19 Seven Hours of Guided Meditation. 142

CONCLUSION 149

Introduction

The word "yoga" has been fascinating us for a very long time. Its literal meaning is "union", which refers to the connection between the physical and the spiritual world. Yoga is a search for the big picture, the real purpose of life, and the knowledge about your own body's energy and full potential. People are interested in yoga because it helps them recognize their inner self and develop consciousness. There are many types of yoga, but the most famous and effective is kundalini yoga. However, we must first discuss the types of yoga that are currently practiced throughout the world. Even though each type of yoga slightly differs in its practices, rituals, and styles, the main goal is always the same. If you decide to take up yoga, you're willing to connect with your inner self and spirituality. The most popular types of yoga in the Western world are:

- Bikram Yoga
- Hatha Yoga
- Ashtanga Yoga
- Hot Yoga
- Kundalini Yoga
- Power Yoga
- Iyengar Yoga
- Vinyasa Yoga
- Prenatal Yoga
- Anusara Yoga
- Yin Yoga
- Jivamukti Yoga
- Shivananda Yoga
- Integral Yoga
- Kripalu Yoga
- Restorative Yoga

- Viniyoga
- Ananda Yoga
- Ishta Yoga
- <u>Strala Yoga</u>
- Svaroopa Yoga
- White Lotus Yoga
- Kali Ray Triyoga
- Acro Yoga
- Kriya Yoga
- Karma Yoga
- Couples Yoga
- Laughter Yoga

In this book, we will briefly discuss all types of yoga you can practice. Then we will discuss kundalini yoga in detail, why it is different, and why you should choose it over all other types of yoga that are available for practice.

What is kundalini yoga? It's believed to be the first form of yoga because it is mentioned in the Upanishads and dates back to 100 BC-500 BC. It mainly consists in finding and experiencing the internal energy present within our physical body. The main goal is to connect with your inner self and awaken the divinity within your body. Now, as you would probably ask, why would you want to do something like this? Why would you need to achieve and recognize your inner energy? Basically, you can achieve complete consciousness, activate your full potential and experience joy, love, and light.

According to the kundalini practice, our energy is not limited within our body, which is just a vessel and carrier of free-flowing energy. The body absorbs and exudes both positive and negative energy. The main goal of kundalini yoga is to experience this flowing energy and consciousness.

Kundalini means 'coiled snake', which is believed to be placed at the base of the spinal cord. In order to experience the full potential of our bodies and divinity, we need to uncoil that snake. It moves through the entire body and the chakras, and it ultimately reaches the center of the forehead; here you can reach the peak of your consciousness, exude energy, and eventually create an aura.

This energy that originates at the base of the spinal cord is associated with feminine energy and is believed to be already present at birth. Therefore, it is not created but is experienced by uncoiling the kundalini. According to the kundalini practice, our body is divided into four chakras. These chakras are the energy centers through which energy flows freely to achieve complete spiritual and divine awakening. Kundalini yoga helps activate these chakras to achieve the highest level of consciousness.

Kundalini yoga incorporates physical poses, breathing techniques, and spiritual chants. The key is consistency; you have to keep on practicing to achieve the desired results.

Chapter 1
The Different Types of Yoga

In this chapter, we will discuss the different types of yoga. However, we must first focus on what yoga is and on the exact meaning of this word.

1.1 Yoga

The word "yoga" is of Sanskrit origin and means "union", which refers to the connection between body and mind. Yogis believe that mind and body are not different entities, and that the ability of the body to perform supremely can only be achieved if it's connected to the mind.

Now we will discuss the most common types of yoga that are practiced predominantly in the United States of America. Below you can find twenty-eight different types of yoga. They are listed based on their popularity according to data collected on the internet.

1.2 Bikram Yoga

This is by far the most famous and practiced type of yoga in North America. Bikram yoga consists in extreme physical exercises and intense kriyas and meditations that are performed in a room at elevated temperatures (95-108 °F). A session usually lasts an hour and a half and focuses on 26 yoga postures. Yoga is a blend of postures, meditations, physical and breathing exercises. The focus is to provide strength to the body. Most people who practice this type of yoga look for body toning and weight loss. Yoga helps strengthen the muscles, and Bikram yoga is extremely effective for arthritis and other aches. Many people who have practiced it have effectively recovered from severe back injuries.

This yoga technique was first taught by teacher Bikram Chaudhry. Since then, it has become a beloved activity in the Western world with approximately 46 000 searches per month.

1.3 Kundalini Yoga

This is the type of yoga we are interested in. Kundalini yoga is quite a famous in the Western world with approximately 39000 searches per month. It is a blend of physical and spiritual practices and incorporates meditations, breathing exercises, and postures. The main focus is to regulate the energy flow through the chakras, and the most important thing is the feminine energy point, which is placed at the base of the spinal cord and contains a lot of sleeping energy. Kundalini yoga tries to wake that energy up and regulate it throughout the body.

In India, the kundalini yoga practice was made popular by Swami Sivanand in the early 1930s. Yogi Bhajan brought Kundalini yoga to the Western world around the late 1960s. Kundalini yoga is most famous among those who are looking for a deeper meaning of life, want to get rid of depression and anxiety, or believe in the process of self-healing through yoga.

Apart from the self-realization and mental strength, one of the most important advantages of kundalini yoga is that it helps with weight loss and prevents some illnesses. Practicing kundalini yoga is good for mental strength and for the nervous system.

This is really helpful for people who are facing problems like anxiety and depression. Kundalini directs the energies in your body in the right direction and makes you feel more at ease. Kundalini yoga is also beneficial for physical diseases such as cholesterol, high blood pressure, and diabetes. Basically, it helps your overall health.

1.4 Hatha Yoga

This is also a famous form of yoga in the United States of America. The internet searches for hatha yoga are around 38000 times per month. This is good for beginners and a gentle and slow type of yoga. The main goal is to achieve flexibility and calm throughout the body. This type of yoga has many benefits for beginners and older people, who cannot perform difficult postures. It also helps with depression, stress relief and flexibility. This type of yoga was found in the 11th century and is similar to Kanphata yoga, which was found by Gorakhnat.

Many other types of yoga take their inspiration from Hatha yoga. It incorporates physical exercises, postures, meditations, and controlled breathing exercises that help you achieve physical and mental balance within your body.

Hatha yoga is beneficial for those who wish to lose a couple of pounds. It might take you more time to lose weight, but in the long run you will find it easier not to gain it again (unlike conventional methods, where all the weight lost comes back if you stop practicing).

1.5 Vinyasa Yoga

This type of yoga dates back to ancient Vedic times and does not have hard or fast rules. The main goal is to find a focus point and balance both mind and body. There are several levels of the vinyasa yoga practice: beginner, intermediate, and intense. This type of yoga is quite famous (32000 searches per month) and helps with blood circulation, stress relief, and overall wellbeing.

Since Vinyasa is easy to practice, a lot of people are interested in it. Practicing Vinyasa yoga helps you relax and maintain a good life-work balance. It provides clarity to the mind, helps with concentration, and regulates the sleep. Vinyasa yoga has also effects on your physical health. As a matter of fact, if you have a healthy mind, your body will be healthy as well.

1.6 Viniyoga

This is another popular type of yoga and is directed more towards healing and therapy. It is specifically designed for treating some acute injuries and chronic conditions. This type of yoga is similar to physical therapy and focuses on long-term healing and quality of life. You can say that Viniyoga is more focused on the long-term effects than on short-term relief.

This type of yoga was developed in the 1970s by Krishnamachariyaa and is really popular among people with approximately 32000 searches per month.

Most Viniyoga classes are group classes, but sometimes individual routines may be offered as well. Yoga exercises and asanas are modified in order not to cause further damage to the already injured or affected parts of the body and to encourage natural healing and stamina building. If you practice Viniyoga, you'll release energy and gain more flexibility and overall strength to the body.

This type of yoga is ideal for people with bone degenerative diseases. For example, people suffering from arthritis and osteoporosis, or those who are recovering from a major physical injury to the spinal cord, or the lower limbs can benefit from Viniyoga. Since its meditations are designed according to one's personal

requirements, choosing this type of yoga is most convenient for people with specific medical and physical requirements. As a matter of fact, Viniyoga is also recommended as a form of physiotherapy after major accidents and injuries.

The benefit of doing yoga is that practices are focused on the mind as well. Practicing yoga clears your mind and gives strength to the brain activity. As a matter of fact, many people suffering from one bone diseases are prone to develop other ailments; this type of yoga helps prevent such things. When the primary ailment is dealt with, there are less chances of more physical problems. Remember that the main goal of yoga is to provide holistic health.

1.7 Ashtanga Yoga

This is another famous type of yoga with about 25000 searches per month. Ashtanga yoga is mainly based on postures and exercises performed in a sequence and focuses on strengthening the core and developing stamina. As with all other kinds of yoga, the main benefits are stress relief, confidence, and clarity of the mind. As a matter of fact, stamina is not limited to physical stamina; Ashtanga yoga helps develop a strong mind as well. It is an advanced-level practice and is not recommended for beginners. This type of yoga was developed in the 20th century by a yoga guru named K. Pittibai Jois.

Ashtanga yoga has a positive effect on both body and mind. Practicing this type of yoga helps you regulate the release of insulin and has a positive effect on the sugar level in the blood. Type 2 diabetes affects almost one third of the USA adult population and may also lead to obesity; therefore, practicing Ashtanga yoga may be really beneficial for those people. Moreover, yoga puts people at ease, which helps a lot while dealing with depression.

1.8 Yin Yoga

This is a relatively new type of yoga and was developed in the early 1970s by Paulie Zink. The main principles of Yin yoga have been inspired by traditional yoga, which roots back to the Hindu religion. However, Yin yoga has a more modern approach and is quite popular in the US with around 24000 searches per month.

Yin yoga is very slow, and most of the exercises are designed to be more relaxed. Maximum breathing and meditation are practiced while sitting or lying down. None of the practices and kriyas last more than five minutes. The main goal of Yin yoga is to strengthen of connective tissues, develop muscle tone, and provide stamina to the skeleton and skeletal muscles.

This type of yoga is mostly practiced by people suffering from arthritis and osteoarthritis and those above the age of 50, who do not want to put pressure on their body beyond its capabilities, while keeping it healthy and strong. Furthermore, Yin yoga brings clarity and peace to the mind and helps with stress and depression.

This is another type of yoga that is directed towards the building up of the muscles and bones. The main goal is to strengthen the basic building structure of the body. As a matter of fact, the exercises are focused on holding the posture and breathing and develop flexibility. As a result, your body will look more toned.

1.9 Iyengar Yoga

This type of yoga is also very popular (16000 searches per month) and was created in the 20th century by Bellur Krishnamachar Sundararaja Iyengar. The basics originate from Hatha yoga, but Iyengar yoga is focused on all areas of wellness. It helps with balance, flexibility, mental and physical strength, and discipline. Practices are focused on the correct postures and breathing exercises, and the main goal is to be as accurate and precise as possible. This type of yoga is most effective on the neck and back and increases the flexibility of the spinal cord and back muscles. Moreover, it has been known to elevate mood, open one's mind to trying new things and become more open to new ideas.

Iyengar Yoga is very popular in many parts of the US, and many studios are opening because of the increasing interest. Iyengar yoga is strict in its rules and regulations, and getting the posture right is the main goal. According to Iyengar yoga beliefs, if you get the correct posture and breathe accurately, you will start getting results in a shorter period of time.

1.10 Restorative Yoga

This is another form of yoga that aims at healing and is known to be quite relaxing. Its popularity has been increasing with time (13000 searches per month). This type of yoga takes inspiration from Iyengar yoga, but it's much more relaxing. It includes deep bending, twisting postures, and breathing exercises. Unlike other types of yoga, you can use pillows and blocks to practice asanas and postures easily.

Restorative yoga has a deep effect on reliving mental stress and making the body more relaxed and the nerves more balanced. Apart from having a positive effect on the mind, practicing restorative yoga helps gain better tone, flexibility, strength, and overall stamina. This yoga is mostly recommended for older people or for those who are recovering from serious health injuries because their body has some restrictions. Restorative yoga techniques, asanas, and meditations are less intense and are designed according to the physical limitations of the students. This kind of yoga has been practiced for many years in India, but it's gaining popularity in the Western world as well.

1.11 Prenatal Yoga

This type of yoga was introduced in the 20th century. It is also relatively popular (12000 per month), considering it was developed for pregnant women. Prenatal yoga can only be performed if you are a yoga expert or under the supervision of a well-trained guru.

Women go through a variety of emotions when they are pregnant. This kind of yoga incorporates easy and effective stretching and breathing exercises that help the mother's mind stay calm and at peace. Prenatal yoga prepares women for childbirth because breathing exercises make their body more flexible, increases stamina, and aligns the energy within the body, which helps with childbirth.

You should always be very careful while practicing prenatal yoga because the body is vulnerable; you should avoid everything that can put the baby in danger. For this reason, prenatal yoga is mostly based on postures and breathing exercises that avoid any risk for both the mother and the baby. However, it's still recommended to practice it under the supervision of a teacher or guru even if you are a yoga expert. During pregnancy it is better to practice yoga only when someone else is around because it's common to have your blood pressure levels fluctuate. Another important point is that you should practice yoga throughout your pregnancy; do not join it in the middle. If you have been doing yoga from the starting months, your body will be more prepared for natural birth without any complications.

1.12 Power Yoga

This type of yoga is based on the Ashtanga style and was created by Beryl Bender Birch. It first became popular in the 1990s, and it is still quite famous to this day (11000 online searches per month). This style is more intense and rigorous, and the main focus is weight loss.

The main techniques are taken from more traditional types of yoga, but the practice is more free flowing. The routines are set like aerobic exercises and focus on weight loss, strength, and stamina. Routines can be performed in any order based on your preferences. Many people looking for weight loss and flexibility find power yoga interesting. Moreover, intense mental exercises are not incorporated, so it's good for people who are not ready for a more spiritual approach to life.

This kind of yoga is more of a physical workout that targets all parts of the body in order to lose weight. Power yoga claims to be the best choice for toning all muscles of the body. It helps you get into shape and also clears the mind of any fogginess and confusion. By practicing power yoga, the cholesterol level decreases within 3 months, and all the internal organs of the body (including the brain and the stomach) are much stronger and more toned.

1.13 Kripalu Yoga

This is a relatively new type of yoga (4000 online searches per month) which was developed around the late 1960s and early 1970s by Amirit Desia. This is a simpler type of yoga that concentrates on providing relaxation to the body. Kripalu Yoga can be practiced by people of all ages and also by those who suffer from chronic illnesses. The main focus is the connection between body and mind, and the exercises are a mix of breathing techniques and postures performed in a relaxed environment. People who practice Kripalu yoga can feel positive, calm, and at peace. Along with the mental benefits, Kripalu yoga also provides flexibility and strength to the body.

1.14 Integral Yoga

This type of yoga was created in the late '60s by Sri Swami Satchidananda. It takes inspiration from all six traditional kinds of yoga, especially from Hatha yoga. Integral yoga predominantly focuses on balancing the mind and body and finding internal peace. Practicing this type of yoga is one of the most relaxing experiences in the world; it gives you inner peace and makes you understand your own needs and desires. Since your chakras are finally unblocked, you can finally be happy. Even though it has a lot of benefits, this type of yoga is not very popular yet (3400 online searches per month).

1.15 Sivananda Yoga

This type of yoga is not very popular and well known (3000 searches per month). It incorporates many kriyas and breathing exercises from Hatha yoga, but it's practiced without music and mantras to help you concentrate. This type of yoga is suitable for people of all ages; however, elderly people should always talk to a doctor before joining any activity because they may have physical problems. Postures and breathing exercises are similar to those practiced in Iyengar yoga, but Sivananda yoga helps with stress relief and sleeping patterns. Overall, it provides a better physical tone and alignment to the body.

1.16 Jivamukti Yoga

This is a relatively new type of yoga created by David Life and Sharon Gannoz in 1994. It's very intense and rigorous and encourages students to practice nonviolence, veganism, and meditation. While practicing it, you will change posture with fluidity. The main goal is to gain a better vision of life and to discover its real meaning, while having an open heart and accepting people despite their differences. Consequently, you can live a happier and purposeful life.

Jivamukti yoga focuses more on lifestyle changes than on physical ones. If you are willing to practice it, be ready to change your entire lifestyle. Meditations and kriyas are based on the traditional principles, but the main goal is to discover the purpose of life. In order to do so, you have to leave everything behind and start with a clean slate. A lot of people can adopt these changes; however, there are also many others who can't keep up with this lifestyle for a long period of time and tend to give up rather quickly.

1.17 Anusara Yoga

Even though Anusara yoga is very effective, it is not very popular (2400 searches per month). It was developed in the nineteen '60s (about the same time as kundalini yoga) and became popular in the '90s thanks to John Friend.

Anusara yoga takes inspiration from Hatha yoga and includes more than fifty asanas. It is very popular among students because the main goal is to calm the nerves and relieve anxiety. Moreover, it aims at developing gratitude and appreciation for life. Anusara yoga mostly focuses on relaxation, meditation, and breathing exercises to keep the mind and body calm and relaxed. This kind of yoga is beneficial for kids because it helps them recognize their emotions and deal with their feelings. In doing so, children will learn to be thankful and be in control of their emotions. Both these qualities are good for life afterwards, and it is better to start working on them at an early age.

Furthermore, Anusara yoga helps with concentration. Children have a very charged up mind, seem to be on the go all the time, and have a small span of attention. Practicing Anusara yoga helps them focus their energies and improve their concentration. Practicing yoga for five to six months can improve their behavior and concentration level. Children can start with yoga classes as soon as they turn five and are able to understand and act on instructions.

This type of yoga is suitable for people of all ages, but if you have a certain medical condition or disease, you should first talk to your doctor. Sometimes even mildest postures or breathing exercises can have a negative effect on your body if you are facing some physical limitations.

1.18 Ishtana Yoga

This is a milder form of yoga that was introduced in South Africa by Yogi Raj Alan Finger and Kavi Yogi Swarnanda Mami Finger in the early 1960s. Father and son had found the benefits of yoga and wanted to spread awareness and knowledge. Even though this type of yoga is yet not very popular in the Western world (2100 searches per month), it's very effective. The main goal is to tell good from bad apart and to work on wellbeing, while developing selflessness and empathy. Ishtana yoga is free-flowing and doesn't have a strict routine or rules, and meditations are designed according to one's needs and abilities. Overall, the main goal is spiritual wellbeing. If you are looking for weight loss and discipline, choose Ishtana yoga because it helps get in shape. There are some intense physical postures and mediations that assure getting a well-toned body with no extra fat. Moreover, you will learn how to follow a routine and develop a more disciplined mind. Practicing this type of yoga for over six months ensures total self-control and excellent concentration. Apart from this, Ishtana yoga has positive effects on your sexual health as well; as a matter of fact, many people practice it to achieve better sexual health and performance. Furthermore, Ishtanga yoga is good for the digestive system and is known to trigger the production of insulin in the blood to keep the sugar levels in control. Due to these benefits, the heart and organ health generally improves.

1.19 Karma Yoga

Karma yoga is quite different from "mainstream" yoga, but it's quite popular (5600 searches per month). It's also one of the most ancient types of yoga and dates back to the time of the Bhagwat Gita. Karma yoga is more about the spiritual side of the yogic techniques and beliefs, but it's based on action rather than on meditation. The concept of Karma is that everything we do has an effect. According to this concept, good actions have a good result, while bad deeds have a bad effect. Therefore, you should concentrate on your Karma and act so that the result of your own actions is also positive. Karma yoga is more about changing your lifestyle, like going for nonviolence and vegetarianism. According to yogic beliefs, each form of living thing is given life with the baggage of their old Karma, and animals could also have been a person in a previous life and have been given this body as a result of their Karma. For this reason, it's forbidden to eat animals and kill any life form. Karma yoga is practiced in all parts of India, and Hindu religion preaches nonviolence and vegetarianism. According to Hindus, if you follow a vegetarian diet routine, you become humbler and more grounded because you eat food cultivated in the soil. Nowadays, many people who practice yoga become vegetarians.

1.20 Couples Yoga

The peculiarity of Couples yoga, which is also very popular in the US (4000 searches per month), is that you have to practice it with a partner. Therefore, it helps with trust-building and sharing energy. This type of yoga is beneficial for new couples because they learn to work together and align their energies. However, it is also practiced by long-term couples as a form of relationship therapy. The main point is to align energies of heart and throat chakras so that the feelings of compassion and love are flow freely. Since most misunderstandings and misconceptions are due to a lack of proper communication, focusing on the throat chakra can help improve communication between partners.

In order to practice Couples yoga, compatibility between partners is absolutely necessary. While practicing, partners learn to appreciate their differences, which is very helpful to the relationship. Moreover, practicing yoga together enhances the feelings of mutual respect and togetherness. Apart from this, the most important aspect of Couples yoga is the sense of belonging, which gives a boost to your confidence and allows you to face the world being more self-assured. Couple yoga can also be really helpful when you are dealing with anger and stress. Couples who practice this type of yoga can also deal with the negative effects of diseases such as high blood pressure, diabetes, and neurodegenerative diseases.

1.21 Laughter Yoga

Laughter yoga was created by Dr. Madan Kataria in 1995, and its main goal is to encourage feelings of happiness and joy. This type of yoga doesn't include any specific exercises or postures, but it aims at keeping the mood light, creating interesting situations, and trigger the laughing, which shouldn't be forced anyway. This is a group activity, and classes take place mostly in groups and outdoors. It is very popular in India, but it's gaining popularity in the Western world as well (2300 searches per month).

It is also believed that Laughter yoga can help with weight loss if you have been practicing it for at least four months. Apart from this, laughing yoga mainly regulates the overall mood, interest in life, selflessness, and sleep.

However, the main goal is to encourage people to laugh. As a matter of fact, laughing triggers endorphins, which in turn induce the feeling of happiness and fulfilment in our bodies and mind. Therefore, laughing also helps with reducing stress and anxiety.

1.22 Acro Yoga

Acro yoga, which was developed in India by Krishnamacharya and is quite famous in the Western world (9200 searches per month), is very intense and based on a combination of asanas and aerobics. In order to practice it, you need to be extremely fit, and you should always be trained by a yogi. You wouldn't want to practice it alone because all asanas are performed while being suspended in the air. Therefore, you need to be assisted by at least two people; while you are performing the asana, another person is holding you, and another one is the spotter. Acro yoga defies gravity and is practiced for the ultimate strength of the mind. In order to practice it, you should be really fit, but you also need to be mentally strong. This is an advanced practice for people who seek extreme concentration and agility of mind, and it's not suitable for beginners. If you don't have an excellent mental control and aren't already physically fit, you shouldn't try it out. However, you can consider watching it because it's marvelous. The benefit of Acro yoga are discipline, mind control, and a higher level of consciousness. Since it requires multitasking and great concentration, all the chakras are affected, and there is a big energy flow.

1.23 Ananda Yoga

Ananda yoga was created around the 1940s and is based on traditional Hatha Yoga. It became popular in the '50s thanks to Kriyananda, who was a student of the guru Paramahasa Yogaandan.

The main goal is to archive the highest level of consciousness and self-awareness. Ananda yoga encourages students to detach themselves from the real world and unplug to find their real purpose in life. Therefore, they will benefit from an overall feeling of wellness and relief from stress and anxiety; moreover, they will become more self-aware and learn to recognize toxic behaviors. This encourages them to become mentally stronger and in much more control of their own lives. This yoga is based on many asanas and meditations that last for a long period of time to build endurance and strength.

Like all other yoga types, Ananda yoga has many benefits. For example, it has a direct effect on the mind and the pituitary gland in the brain and helps tone both the hemispheres of the brain. Moreover, it is very helpful for the digestive system. Most of the time, the major cause of digestive problems is anxiety; since Ananda yoga helps relieve stress, it has a positive effect on the digestive system as well. People who are suffering from flatulence and heartburn should follow Ananda yoga to get relief from these symptoms.

1.24 Kriya Yoga

This is also an ancient type of yoga and dates back to thousands of years ago. However, it became really popular around 1861 thanks to Mahavatar, who practiced it while he was in the Himalayas. Nowadays, it's quite popular in the Western world (7800 searches per month).

As the name suggests, Kriya yoga is based on rituals, physical exercises, and postures; it includes kriyas and meditations for short intervals to gain mental peace and calm. Its main goal is to strengthen both body and mind while focusing on the spinal cord. According to tradition, the lower part of the spinal cord is the base of energy; therefore, you should strengthen it.

People who practice Kriya yoga have a strong spine and are really flexible. Moreover, if you have been practicing it regularly for five or six months, you tend to become humbler and more empathetic. Additionally, you develop a strong mindset and become more confident.

1.25 Strala Yoga

The meaning of the word "strala" is "radiating light". This type of yoga is related to traditional Chinese medicine, tai chi, and qi gong. This type of yoga was created by Micheal Taylor and Tara Stiles in 2008, so it's relatively new and not very popular yet (700 searches per month).

Strala yoga focuses on positively impacting one's overall health and helps with stress relief and anxiety. The main goal is to keep the stress levels low and to follow a healthier lifestyle. Since it incorporates Chinese medicine, it is also a healing type of yoga.

Strala yoga has an effect on the overall mental and physical health, and it's usually practiced to strengthen the mind. It has been found that it is very effective for people suffering from anxiety and PTSD, and it can also help while dealing with degenerative diseases such as dementia and Alzheimer's. Apart from having a positive effect on mental health, it also helps regulate insulin and blood sugar. This type of yoga has also an effect on the overall mood and help regulate the sleep patterns if you practice it consistently for three-four months. You should try this type of yoga if you are suffering from any sort of mild anxiety and depression. However, if you are facing some serios mental or physical disorders, you should always talk to your doctor before starting any yoga practice. Same goes for medication; if you are on certain medication, you should inform your doctor beforehand.

1.26 Svaroopa Yoga

This type of yoga is based on ancient practices and is gaining more and more popularity in the Western world (1500 searches per month) because it's relatively easy and has a lot of benefits.

Svaroopa yoga incorporates traditional meditations, kriyas, asanas, and mudras; however, you can also use accessories that help you (e.g., soft blocks, blankets, pillows). Therefore, anyone can practice it (even those suffering from arthritis), and it's especially recommended for beginners.

The pioneer of Svaroopa yoga was Swamin Nirmalandada Saraswati, who wanted to include everyone to the mystic experience of yoga. Many people are afraid to join yoga because they think their bodies are not flexible enough; due to this kind of pressure, they end up not trying at all. For such people, Svaroopa yoga is the best option because they can use pillows and blocks. If you feel accomplished, you are encouraged to push your body further; in no time, you realize that your body is flexible enough to try more difficult exercises.

Svaroopa yoga was also created while having in mind people with physical limitations, who shouldn't feel excluded. Some research has found that the use of pillows and bocks does not decrease the effects and the efficacy of yoga; even with the help of blocks and blankets, you can achieve good results.

1.27 White Lotus Yoga

White lotus yoga, which is not very famous yet (400 searches per month), is based on ancient yoga traditions and mainly focuses on meditation and breathing. It incorporates breathing control and systemic breathing with specific postures. These meditations are especially beneficial for opening the heart chakra, which helps the lungs and respiratory system.

This type of yoga was developed in the 1960s by Ganga White. It is beginner-level yoga and is suitable for people of all ages. However, if you suffer from a specific physical condition, you should consult a doctor beforehand.

White Lotus yoga is beneficial for people who are dealing with mild psychological conditions such as anger management and anxiety. Practicing controlled breathing activates the pituitary gland, which releases enzymes that strengthen the control centers of the body. As a result, the overall mood improves while practicing White lotus yoga. Young kids should practice it to gain total control of their emotions and desires by the time they get older.

1.28 Kali Ray Triyoga

Kali Ray Triyoga is still not very popular in the Western world (60 searches per month). It is based on Hatha yoga and was created by Kali Ray. It includes flowing postures and breathing exercises, and the main goal is to generate a flexible and flowing movement of the spinal cord, which ensures the free flow of energy throughout the body. This flow creates a positive mindset and helps relieve tension. Moreover, it encourages the opening of the heart and throat chakra, which leads the student to become more open and accepting. One of the main benefits of this type of yoga is that those who practice it gain self-confidence and get rid of anxiety. Practicing Kali Ray yoga over time changes your perception of life as a whole, and you become much more positive.

If you keep practicing this type of yoga, you will realize it is more like a dance routine. The dancing movements and rhythm created in the body will encourage the secretion of endorphins, which makes you feel happy and fulfilled.

In this chapter we had a look at many different types of yoga practiced throughout the world. Our main focus was to learn in detail about forms that originate in ancient India. Apart from these, there are also ancient Chinese techniques which use the same principles as yoga to incorporate balance and strength to the body. The most famous in the Western world is tai chi, which is known to be effective in healing body blockages related to the sinuses and the digestive system.

Chapter 2
Types of Energy

When we talk about yoga, one main topic is always energy. But what is this energy? Where does it originate from? How can this energy be used? This chapter will answer all these questions. The four types of energy we will discuss in this chapter are:

- Kundalini
- Dharma
- Karma
- The nature of prana

2.1 Kundalini Energy

What exactly is kundalini energy? We know it's represented by a coiled snake at the base of our spines and as a feminine type of energy. According to some scriptures, the coiled snake is present in the human body from the time of birth; then we go through puberty, and that's the time when kundalini energy is released. The activation of kundalini energy causes all the emotional and physical changes that you experience during puberty. According to yogic tradition, there are two types of energy: Shiva and Shakti. Shiva is the masculine energy and the spiritual power. On the other hand, Shakti, which means "energy" or "power", is the physical power we experience while living in the world. According to yogic beliefs, when the kundalini shakti is combined with its masculine counterpart, you experience a state of full consciousness, mental clarity, and truth known as a kundalini awakening.

Kundalini awakening has been mentioned in many ancient

scriptures such as the Upanishads and is achieved through deep meditation and concentration. However, there is no sure way to experience it. The compatibility between the feminine and the masculine energy is necessary to trigger the kundalini awakening. It is believed that the kundalini awakening causes the cells in the body to renew and regenerate. It also sends signals through the neurons to other parts of the body to trigger the active healing processes. This gives a renewed power to both body and mind. In order to experience kundalini awakening, our soul must be mature enough to understand changes occurring in body and mind. This is why you should never rush this process; your soul must be mature enough to deal with the rapid changes and the infinite state of consciousness.

Kundalini is a high-frequency energy represented by seven layers and seven sub-layers. When the kundalini awakens, you can feel it very intensely. Only if kundalini awakening is achieved properly, the body can deal with this enormous level of energy. If you force the process, you might experience negative effects known as the kundalini syndrome (e.g., hallucinations, hot flashes, crying, body pain, and fevers). Therefore, you should always practice kundalini yoga with a trained guru who can guide you throughout it.

2.2 Dharma

According to yogic philosophy, Dharma is the energy that drives the universe and is based on some principles that you should follow during your life. The law of Dharma has also been called the law of the righteous or the path of truth. According to Hindu religion, the Dharma is the right path you must follow to create an energy aura. Specifically, you have to behave well and be selfless because good actions and devotion are one of the main key concepts of yoga. In other words, following Dharma is the correct way to live your life.

If we go into the deep meaning of the word, we will find out that "Dharma" derives from "dhiri", which means "to keep in the original condition" or "to keep order". Dharma is the cosmic law that upholds the universe and prevents destruction. Therefore, everyone should follow it so that the world around them stays ordered and chaos is prevented.

2.3 Karma

As you may know, the word "Karma" is commonly used with different meanings. While reading, you will learn how our intentions, desires, and feelings affect our behavior and actions, and how this is also related to Karma. First of all, "Karma" is a Sanskrit word that means "action" and describes all our physical and mental actions. Karma is also said to mirror what's happened in the past and what will happen in the future. In general, daily activities such as going to work, doing good deeds, kindness etc., all are also called Karma. Everything you do now is the result of what you have done before; therefore, whatever you are experiencing in your life right now results from your earlier intentions and depends on karmic bonds.

Because of our Karmas, we constantly fall in the cycle of births. In other words, our experiences of happiness and sorrow are always the result of Karma charged or accumulated in our previous lives. Even after achieving self-realization, you can live happily with all your behavior as now. After gaining knowledge, there is no bondage of any kind, and only knowledge is attained in the future. The ultimate salvation is attained when all the karmas are over. Life has given us all the keys to understanding how Karma works in a very simple way. The fruit of Karma is not a punishment or reward, but it depends on our own intentions.

The karma seeds sown in the previous birth grow into fruits in this birth. But who would give you this fruit? God? No, we naturally experience the fruits of Karma at the right time. Ignoring our nature the root cause of a new Karma being charged. Everything we experience is our creation, and no one is responsible for it; we are solely responsible for our eternal births. Many people believe that everything they experience in life is their own. So, they try to change it but fail because it is not in their hands to change it completely. It is right to change the fruit, but are they fully capable of doing this? Yes, but to some extent. They do not have much control over it. This is possible only after attaining enlightenment; it is not possible until then. If so, then... Can you use this knowledge to achieve you goal? Can you get rid of your Karma before it has any negative effect? Could it be that you do not bind Karma and experience your state of self-bliss even after living your life as normal? Can you be freed from the bondage of your eternal births?

2.4 The Nature of Prana

The literal meaning of "Orana" is "force that drives life", which is represented by our breathing. If our body is breathing, we are considered alive; on the contrary, once the breathing stops, our physical body is considered lifeless and dead. According the yogic philosophy, Prana is the energy driving the entire body and is represented by the five senses:

- Sense of Smell
- Sense of Sight
- Sense of Touch
- Sense of Hearing
- Sense of Taste.

All these senses are controlled by a single primary source of life which is breathing. A person with no breath is lifeless; on the contrary, someone who has lost their senses but still breaths is considered alive.

When we talk about Prana, we mean the force driving energy and creativity in our body that also plays a big role in the practice of kundalini yoga. There are five types of Pranas:

- Prana Vayu

"Prana Vayu" literally means "air that is moving forward".

Therefore, Prana Vayu includes everything the body receives through itself such as the air we inhale, the water we drink, the food we eat, the voices we hear, and the fragrances we smell.

It represents our three body systems: respiratory system, ear canal, and digestive system. First of all, we have the respiratory system, which is connected to the air that is inhaled to bring life to the body. It also represents the sense of smell, which is the strongest of the five senses. As a matter of fact, it's widely known that people associate feelings with smell. For example, if you had a good time with your family at a new coffee shop, you will always associate the smell of coffee with family and happy times. Similarly, smells could be associated with negative feelings. For example, imagine that you picked a rose to smell it, but you accidentally touch a thorn; as a result, whenever you smell a rose, you will always associate it with pain.

The next system associated with Vayu is the ear canal, and so the sense of hearing. Voice is basically air flowing in your ears. However, if you understand the meaning of what other people are saying, you can connect and really communicate with them.

Last but not the least is the digestive system until the stomach. It represents food and water absorbed by the body. Energy taken from food and water is transformed into another type of energy and provides nourishment to the body. Therefore, eating healthy food also means receiving positive energy that can be transformed into good energy for the body. This goes on to prove the philosophy of kundalini: Energy keeps changing and getting into one movement throughout the day.

- Udana Vayu

"Udana Vayu" means "air that moves in the upward direction" and refers to life constantly changing and moving in the right direction, which refers to growth both in size and in wisdom.

Udana Vayu is the representation of the most basic characteristic of living things: growth. After a child is born, he starts growing from day one. The word "Udana Vayu" also signifies "upwards and outwards", which means that you always grow in the upward direction. For example, you grow taller as you become older. Similarly, Udana Vayu represents the mental growth and growth in wisdom.

- Samana Vayu

"Samana Vayu" means "balancing air" and refers to all the processes taking place within our body, such as blood circulation, the digestion of food to create energy, and the exchange of air in the lungs to provide oxygen to all parts of the body.

- Apana Vayu

The literal meaning of "Apana Vayu" is "air that is moving away", which refers to everything that is eliminated from the body. The excretory system and the reproductive system represent the Apana Vayu. The excretory system includes the digestive system from the stomach to the anus, which also means that it represents toxic materials and negativity that you need to eliminate from your body. Therefore, Apana Vayu refers to the removal of physical waste from the body as well as to the spiritual removal of negative energies.

However, not everything that is removed from the body is necessarily negative. As a matter of fact, the reproductive system represents the creation of positive energy through childbirth. It is also believed that childbirth is sometimes so intense that some women experience a full-fledged kundalini awakening during it. Therefore, birth is considered sacred in the kundalini yoga practice because this new energy that can be created means that life goes on.

- Vyana Vayu

"Vyana Vayu" refers to the air moving outwards, and so it's connected to the respiratory and circulatory systems, which also include nose, larynx, pharynx, and lungs. Vyana Vayu is the most important type of Prana. The breath that we exhale represents the toxicity and the negativity that we expel from our bodies and minds.

If you practice yoga, you should always pay attention to Prana because it's really important. According to the ancient beliefs, all human beings are born with energy within themselves. This energy takes physical form and changes shape, but it's never completely destroyed. As we already discussed, Prana refers to breathing and plays a big role in kundalini yoga. As a matter of fact, this type of yoga incorporates different breathing exercises in order to control the course of life. Moreover, it describes all power and energy that can be found in the human body and produce change in our lives.

Chapter 3
The Five Elements in Yoga

According to yoga, there are five natural elements that are related to body and nature and have an impact on our physical and mental well-being. They are known as Pancha tattva in Sanskrit. By aligning their energies, we can intensify the effects they have on our lives. According to yogic philosophy, some human features are associated with natural elements, and so are chakras. In order to benefit from them, we have to focus on that certain parts of our bodies and meditate using mudras and kriyas. It is also believed that certain food can also stimulate the alignment between these energy centers and natural elements.

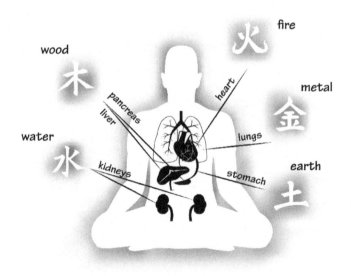

The five natural elements will be discussed in detail in the following chapter and are:

- Fire Element (Agni tattva)
- Water Element (Jal tattva)
- Earth Element (Prithvi tattva)
- Ether Element (Akasha tatva)
- Air Element (Vayu tattva)

3.1 Fire Element

The fire element is the primary source and center of light, heat, and warmth. It is connected to the third chakra (solar plexus chakra) and represents the soul. The fire element represents our physical well-being and nourishment. Therefore, it's involved in the process where we absorb energy from food and provide it to our body. If you experience indigestion, heartburn, flatulence, and gases, you may have some problems with the fire element. However, you can easily solve it by performing specific asanas directed towards the solar plexus.

When it comes to mental well-being, the fire element represents our thinking and changes in perception that occur during our lives. It shows our ability to navigate through changes, and what these experiences bring to our lives. Now, if you feel anxiety and fear and cannot let go of your past or deal with change, it may be because your fire element is blocked. This problem can easily be solved thanks to asanas that restore the free flow of energy.

3.2 Water Element

Water is associated with fluidity and free flow, and so with emotions and feelings. The water element is located in the second chakra (sacral chakra), and cleansing and clearing organs like kidneys, bladder, and those associated with childbirth are all related to it. As a matter of fact, it allows the body to clear and cleanse from toxicity (both physical and mental). Drinking a lot and eating food rich in water encourages keeping the water element aligned, while beneficial asanas are those that allow the opening of the pelvic bone.

3.3 Earth Element

The earth element is associated with the first chakra (root chakra) and keeps you grounded and connected to your life purpose. Earth represents stability and is associated with keeping work and life in balance. In order to do so, you should relax and spend time in nature. Moreover, you should practice asanas directed to the root chakra and eat a lot of cereals, meat, nuts, and root vegetables.

3.4 Ether Element

The ether element is also known as space element and is related to the throat chakra. It represents one's mind and awareness. The opening and alignment of this element help you gain consciousness, open up to new ideas, and get out of your comfort zone. As mind does not have any shape and cannot be contained somewhere, this element represents unlimited possibilities and creativity.

3.5 Air Element

Air element is connected to the heart chakra and represents the free flow of air, that is breathing (Prana). The air element is associated with unconditional love, compassion, and empathy.

In order to keep it aligned, it is recommended to perform breathing exercises and asanas because they will open up your chakra and help you feel fulfilled.

Chapter 4
The Four Paths of Yoga

While practicing yoga, the ultimate goal is gaining self-awareness, peacefulness, and happiness. According to yogic tradition, your inner self is represented by Atma, which derives from the supreme self (Paramatma). The goal of Paramatma is to achieve ultimate happiness, which is known as Ananda. Essentially, yoga guides you towards Ananda so that you can reach ultimate happiness and contentment. The happiness you are looking for is not from the outside world, but from your inner body. According to yogic tradition, you can follow four paths to achieve unlimited happiness.

- Bhakti yoga
- Karma yoga
- Raja yoga
- Jnana yoga

However, you should pay attention. People often think they can choose the path on their own, but this is a misconception. All the paths actually go hand in hand and lead to the ultimate goal of peace and happiness. In general, they describe the lifestyle you should adopt to achieve this ultimate goal.

4.1 Bhakti Yoga

"Bhakti" means "devotion". According to this practice, you should devote yourself to the supreme power, take care of nature, and love animals, plants, and human beings.

Every religion implies the existence of a supreme power. Hinduism has many gods, but the main one is the most powerful and has created this universe. Bhakti is the devotion to that supreme power; you can make it happy if you take care of nature, animals, and fellow human beings. In general, Bhakti yoga is a lifestyle of devotion and service to the mankind. Therefore, you are encouraged to give up meat, avoid showing aggression, and protest against torture. What you should always remember is that Bhakti yoga is strictly non-violent.

4.2 Karma Yoga

"Karma" means "action", and here's the thing: Every kind of action will have a specific reaction as a result. Therefore, whatever is happening to you is a reaction of something you did or thought.

Karma yoga is the yoga of doing. It includes all sorts of kriyas, asanas, and breath control exercises. By practicing mudras and meditation, you get a fitter body and a sharper mind as a result.

4.3 Raja Yoga

This is the most familiar type of yoga for us and is also known as the royal path of yoga. This includes self- awareness and discipline. You will practice meditation, kriyas, asanas, and breathing exercises to become physically stronger, more self-aware, and disciplined. However, it also deals with controlling your emotions and gaining mental stability.

The main benefit of Raja yoga is that it has a direct effect on the clarity of mind and soul. While practicing it, you will become able to live in the moments, let go of people who hurt you and radiate positive vibes and energy.

4.4 Jnana Yoga

In general, yoga aims at gaining more self- awareness and knowledge. Jnana yoga's main goal is to distinguish between what's real and what is not.

This is also what you must keep in mind while practicing kundalini yoga; you are working to achieve the highest level of knowledge and consciousness. In order to recognize your real purpose in life, you should try Jnana yoga. It has many physical benefits, but it mostly affects your mind.

But pay attention; these four paths are not types of yoga. They have the same goal and are connected to each other. While practicing whichever type of yoga, you are either simultaneously treading on all four paths or you are taking one path at a time. No matter what the sequence is, the main goal is always the same.

Chapter 5
The Basics of Kundalini Yoga

Now that you got to know yoga and its benefits on the body, mind, and soul, let's focus on Kundalini yoga. What is it exactly? Like all other types of yoga, Kundalini yoga is based on the connection between body and mind. However, it focuses on the uncoiling of the divine energy located at the base of the spine. As a matter of fact, the literal meaning of "kundalini" is "coiled snake". It is believed that when you are born, your body has an unlimited amount of energy that is coiled under the spinal cord. The main goal of kundalini yoga is to uncoil it to ensure the free flow of energy throughout the body up until the crown chakra. In doing so, body and mind are connected to the divine energy symbolized by the Kundalini Shakti.

Kundalini yoga is an ancient practice that aims at healing mind and soul. It awakens the energy centers in the body, connects them to the divine energy, makes you experience unlimited love, clear mind, and happiness, and makes sure that you reach your full potential.

Whatever we experience in life and whoever we meet is a form of positive and negative energy transfer. Yoga teaches us how to absorb this energy in the most effective way.

Kundalini yoga is a type of yoga that combines physical exercises, mental chants, and mantras to reach this point. Now you may ask whether this practice works and how it actually affects body and mind. According to yogic beliefs, all the energy that a person requires is generated from within the body. The only problem is that sometimes the energy centers, which are seven and allow energy to flow freely throughout the body, are blocked, and energy is most helpful when it flows throughout the body. Kundalini yoga provides the framework to achieve this neutral mind space. The specific asanas and mantras trigger and stimulate the energy centers within the body to achieve a state of calm and peace.

We often experience ups and downs and stress because life is fast paced nowadays. Kundalini yoga helps us focus our energy through our body by uncoiling the energy placed at the base of our spine. Therefore, all energy centers will be unlocked, and energy can flow throughout the body, keeping it in balance. Moreover, Kundalini yoga has positive effects on physical strength and flexibility.

After kundalini yoga arrived in the Western world, it has been done detailed scientific research on the topic; it has been proved that it directly affects the nervous system at the cellular level. Practicing it continuously and with a consistent routine stimulates the nervous system, reinforcing positive effects on the mind. Kundalini yoga really helps with weight loss, arthritis, depression, and stress control.

Teachers and gurus often wear white dresses and headgears. Although it is not compulsory to wear white or even the headcover, it is believed that each color has its energy and affects consciousness. The energy emitted or absorbed by different colors might be negative or positive, might interfere with the attainment of enlightenment, and could interrupt the flow of energy throughout the body. White is believed to be the purest color and acts as a mirror to reflect and absorb energy. Wearing white means that your body can do so without interfering with the consciousness. Gurus might also wear a white turban on their heads. This also symbolizes purity and helps to focus the energy at the chakra placed at the third eye level. Chakras and energy centers are explained in the following chapters of the book, in which we will also discuss kundalini yoga practices in detail.

5.1 Five Basic Aspects of Kundalini Yoga

Now let's focus more on kundalini yoga practice. It's basically a mix of physical exercises and meditation and includes five main things:

- Breath Work

Mantras

- Kriyas
- Meditation
- Mudras

They are different, but they're also equally beneficial. We are now discussing each one in detail.

- Breath Work

Breath work is an essential part of kundalini yoga; as a matter of fact, this type of yoga is based on deep breathing. First you slowly inhale through your nose to fill up your lungs, while your stomach is expanding; then you slowly exhale and squeeze your stomach until lungs are empty. Deep breathing is beneficial to control stress and anxiety. It can be practiced at any time of the day, and for as short as two minutes, you will be able to relax and calm down. In order to practice it correctly, you have to put your left hand on your heart and your right hand on your stomach.

Moreover, kundalini yoga incorporates the breath of fire. You have to quickly inhale and exhale while pumping your stomach to provide oxygen through the blood. As a result, the electromagnetic field around your aura becomes more intense. The breath of fire instantly gives you more energy, and you feel a rush of blood throughout your body.

Mantras

At first, mantras may be intimidating. However, they are nothing to be scared of. It is believed that each sound stimulates a chemical signal within the brain. As a result, it produces specific hormones, and you instantly feel positive and happy. When you chant, the sound resonates with a certain frequency, making the body vibrate and releasing positive energy. It is also believed that chanting makes your body connect with higher frequencies, improves your mood, and balances your mind. Moreover, it also attracts positive energy from your surroundings. When it comes to mantras, there are no strict rules. For example, you can practice them while driving, sitting, or cooking in your house. This chanting connects you to divinity.

- Kriyas

"Kriya" literally means "action". In order to do an action, you have to combine breathing, asanas, and mantras. Only while practicing a kriya, you can get the full potential and benefits of kundalini yoga. In order to do so, you must focus on three parts of your body: the mind, the physical body, and the connection with spirit or soul. The main goal is to achieve a life full of strength, abundance, prosperity, and full potential. You can simply sit down with your legs crossed in the lotus pose; now close your eyes, stretch out your arms and place them on your knees, join the middle finger and thumb in a mudra, and practice deep breathing. This one of the simplest kriyas and is known as the balancing kriya.

- Mudras

Mudras are the hand gestures used in most types of yoga. They are meant to direct energy to a specific part of the brain. It is believed that pressing specific parts of your body with your fingers triggers a certain energy center, directs energy to the brain, and stimulates it to release that energy.

One of the most common mudras is the Gyan mudra, which literally means "knowledge". It is practiced to make you mind stronger and retain knowledge. All you need to do is pressing the pad of the index finger to the pad of the thumb and applying pressure with all other fingers open. Another common mudra is very helpful if you wish to relieve stress and anxiety, perhaps before a big presentation or during a meeting. In this case, you must push the pinky finger nail into the pad of the thumb, apply pressure for one minute, and then release. This will help you calm down your nerves and gain more self-assurance and confidence.

5.2 The Four Body Locks

Kundalini yoga only includes a few postures. These are the four locks and are used in most meditations to direct energy to the third eye. These body locks help with the healing process and make you feel calm and peaceful. They energize both your physical body and your spirits. Below they are mentioned in both their traditional and their English name, but later on you'll only find them mentioned in English:

- Jalandhar Bandha (neck lock)
- Mul Bandha (root lock)
- Uddiyana Bandha (diaphragm lock)
- Maha Bandha (great lock)

Each lock is performed in specific meditations and kriyas and has its own benefits.

- Neck Lock

The neck lock is the most common one. It's used in most Pranama and other simple meditations, and regulates the soft and subtle movements of the upper part of the body. All you have to do is lifting the chest and sternum; after that, move the chin towards the back of your neck to lengthen it and relax your neck, face, and throat muscles. You can practice it while holding your breath or exhaling. It also helps regulate hormonal secretions, clears the mind, and calms the heart by directing energy to the central channel.

- Root Lock

This lock is performed at the root chakra level and works as a hydraulic lock. It regulates energies of the lower triangle of the body, including the lower three chakras. The main goal is to balance the energy of the sexual organs, rectum, and navel area. The root lock helps you feel sexual energy and desire in a more controlled way while energy flows through the body. You must squeeze the anal sphincter and sex organs' muscles; then you must pull your navel towards your spine simultaneously. The most important benefit of this lock is the proper and regulated flow of the cerebrospinal fluid. You can perform it only after specific meditations and kriyas, and you can choose to hold your breath or to exhale. However, women shouldn't perform this lock when they are on their period.

- Diaphragm Lock

This is a relatively difficult lock for beginners, and you should be very careful while performing it. Remember to start all the locks and meditations with short intervals, gradually increasing intensity. As a matter of fact, if you force your body beyond its limits, you could hurt yourself, and healing could take a long time. The body transforms itself gradually and at a slow pace. If yours is stiff and not flexible enough, just take your time and keep training to become more and more flexible.

If you are ready to perform this lock, take a deep breath to inhale and then fully exhale air from your body. Then pull the stomach and abdominals towards the spine, but do not pull back your navel area. At this point, you will notice that your navel area will move upwards. If you are performing it while standing, your legs should be slightly apart and equal to the width of your shoulders. Then bend forward with your back straight and your hands on your knees. In this position, the lock can be performed more easily. Once you have performed it, you will feel a slight tightening at the base of your throat. While holding your breath out, hold this position for ten seconds and gradually increase intensity to one minute. Now slowly get back to a normal position, take a deep breath to fill your lungs, and then exhale slowly to empty them. Remember not to perform this lock after meals and make sure that your stomach is empty.

This lock is difficult to perform, but it has so many benefits. It massages the hearth, the intestines, and the stomach. It also improves your skin and energy. Moreover, it helps with verbal expression, opens up the heart chakra, and stimulates positive feelings of passion, compassion, forgiveness, and empathy.

- Great Lock

When the neck, the root, and the diaphragm lock are performed simultaneously, the result is the great lock. If you are a beginner, it may be difficult for you to perform it. Therefore, you should first practice and master all other locks.

The great lock is performed throughout many meditations and kriyas and helps with many diseases and ailments such as blood pressure and indigestion. It's also beneficial for hormonal flow regulation and for those who have menstrual cramps. However, you should not perform it if you are on you period.

Chapter 6
The History of Kundalini Yoga

It's widely known that kundalini yoga is one of the most ancient if not the most ancient type of yoga.

Even though we don't actually know its exact history, it is believed that kundalini yoga originated before other types of yoga. As a matter of fact, it has been found that Egyptians practiced something similar to kundalini. Moreover, there is evidence that the ancient Chinese and the Native Americans also performed similar rituals. What all these practices have in common is that they focus on the energy located at the end of the spinal cord and associated with feminine energy. Throughout history, this feminine energy has been celebrated and believed to be connected to life and reproduction. Kundalini works the same way because it focuses on releasing this feminine energy to achieve the highest level of consciousness and reach the full potential of the human body.

Some archeologists also found wall paintings portraying yoga-like postures in cities located in the Indus Valley (e.g., Mohenjo Daro and Harrapa). They date back to 5000 years ago, and this is around the same time when Eastern religion and philosophy were found. We can find parallel teachings between the yogic practices and the Eastern religion, which is focused on the search for divinity and the spiritual connection with the physical body. However, according to other historians, kundalini yoga could be traced back to 8000 years ago. In any case, it's proven that it has been practiced for thousand years.

Before incorporating physical exercises, yoga was probably first created as spiritual and philosophical training. There is written evidence of this in the Vedas found in the Upanishads. The literal meaning of the word "Upanishads" is "to listen to the teaching of the spiritual teacher". In the Upanishads, yoga is described both as the study and science of power and energy and as the connection between the physical body and the spirit. Therefore, it can be said that the study and knowledge of yoga have played an important part in Hindu religion for a long time.

Yogic teachings and practices might have been found before the Hindu religion, but the preservation of this art and philosophy was started by Hindu yogis. Moreover, yogic knowledge and practice have always been considered sacred and divine and didn't spread beyond the Eastern world for a long time. It was transferred from guru to students as a sacred trust and considered holy and very important. This is one of the main reasons why kundalini yoga is relatively new to the Western world. This knowledge had been purposely kept a secret.

In the Western world, yoga was first introduced in the 20th century by Sir John Woodruffe, a scholar of Hindu philosophy. However, kundalini yoga only gained popularity in US at the end of the 1960s.

A man named Yogi Bhajan was a yogi from Punjab, India. He was well aware that yoga was a well-kept secret and was not to be shared in the Western world. However, while on a trip to Los Angeles, he completely changed his mind. He realized that something as sacred as yoga should be available to all human beings. It is a birthright of all humans to experience the full potential, calmness of mind and body, and reach the highest level of enlightenment. He felt that each one should get a chance to fully enjoy life. It was 1968; around the same time the hippie movement was becoming stronger and stronger, and young people were looking for enlightenment and the highest state of consciousness. Yogi Bhajan realized that these people were not on the right path; their goal was valid, but their manners weren't correct. At this point, he decided to start spreading his knowledge of kundalini yoga. Throughout his life, he taught more than 8000 classes and found an organization named "The three Hs" (Happy, Healthy and Holy Organization). By the year 1969, he had started yoga teacher training courses as well. Many of his trained teachers, including Gurmut Kaur, found studios in Canada and in the US. Moreover, he wrote many books about spirituality and enlightenment and established World Peace Day. He even collaborated with governments to promote peace through yoga.

In the Western world, Kundalini yoga is going strong as ever. With kundalini yoga studios located in all major cities in the United States, people are trying to experience the yogic way of life and are quite satisfied and convinced with its teaching and philosophy.

Chapter 7
The Chakras

In this chapter, we will focus on the seven chakras. In order to understand kundalini yoga and yoga in general, we must first learn the terminology as well. In modern-day yoga practice, most of the words have been translated to English. However, it is essential to use the correct terminology and know the meaning of these words to fully experience yoga. Throughout the yoga practice, you will find a theme to gain fulfillment and reach the full potential of the human body. When we talk about the human body, we must consider it both physically and mentally. Sometimes we forget the soul, and so we do not understand what the human body is really capable of. Kundalini yoga helps you reach your full potential and makes it easier for you to realize who you really are and what you can do.

Now let's focus on chakras. The literal meaning of "chakra" is "full circle" or "spinning wheel". As a matter of fact, chakras are symbolized by a spinning wheel. But what are chakras exactly? Let's take a look at them. According to the yogic beliefs, body is not merely a physical entity; it is also packed with free-flowing energy. This energy is concentrated in seven main points of the human body, which are called chakras.

Each chakra plays a specific role and is connected to specific functions, needs, and desires. In order to make sure that energy flows freely throughout the body, you have to focus on specific chakras. However, most of the time, they are blocked, and so is the free flow of energy. Kundalini meditations make it easier to unblock chakras and allow the free flow of energy throughout the body. The ultimate goal is to open the crown chakra, which is located at the top of the head and symbolizes thought, consciousness, and wisdom.

The following chart gives a brief overview of the seven chakras, their English and traditional names, their location in the body, and asanas to activate them. It has already been said that chakras are energy centers. According to the yogic practice, they are also points where physical body, energy, thoughts, and feelings meet. How we experience life and how we react to certain situations is reflected by these spinning wheels. The energy flowing through the chakras represents our behaviors, our tone of speaking, our level of confidence, and even our physical symptoms.

YOGIC CHAKRA GUIDE	ASANA
7: **Crown Chakra** (*Sahasrara*): "To Know"	Sirasana Sasangasana Padmasana
6: **Third Eye** (*Ajna*): "To Perceive"	Balasana
5: **Throat Chakra** (*Vishuddha*): "To Speak"	Sarvangasana Halasana Matsyasana
4: **Heart Chakra** (*Anahata*): "To Love"	Ushtrasana Urdhva Mukha svanasana Marjaryasana
3: **Solar Plexus Chakra** (*Manipura*): "To Act"	Virabhadrasana (1,2,3) Navasana Dhanurasana Urdhva hastasana
2: **Sacral Chakra** (*Swadhisthana*): "To Feel"	Baddha konasana Utkata konasana Kapotasana
1: **Root Chakra (Muladhara)**: "To Have"	Tadasana Malasana Setu Bandha Salabhasana

Each chakra has its own symbol, is associated with a natural element and a color, and controls specific emotions and body functions. In order to activate a specific chakra, you have to perform specific asanas and exercises.

Furthermore, chakras can be divided into three categories:

- The lower triangle
- The balance-point
- The upper triangle

The lower triangle deals with the first three chakras and with the physical needs of the body. Chakras associated with the lower triangle are:

1. Muladhara (Root Chakra)
2. Swadhisthana (Sacral Chakra)
3. Manipura (Solar Plexus Chakra)

The balance point is connected to the heart chakra (Anahata, or heart chakra), and so to heart and soul. It is mostly associated with selfless service and forgiveness.

The upper triangle is associated with our relationship with divinity and the self-consciousness. The three chakras associated with the upper triangle are:

1. Visshuddha (Throat Chakra)
2. Ajna (Third Eye Chakra)
3. Sahasrara (Crown Chakra)

7.1 Muladhara, the Root Chakra

This is the first chakra and is really important because it is the focal point of the feminine energy. The Kundalini Shakti is believed to be the feminine energy located at the base part of the pelvic floor and is represented as a coiled snake. In order to activate it, you must practice meditation and kriya constantly. Basically, that's how the kundalini yoga practice begins.

The root chakra is located between the anal sphincter and sexual organs at the base of the spine. Therefore, it is associated with the element of earth and deals with basic needs such as survival, food, sleep, and sex. It helps the body remain grounded and control the physical urges that drive it, but it's also associated with doubts, confidence, fear, and attempts to avoid difficult situations. While practicing the poses and meditations to strengthen the root chakra, you won't be able to totally control your physical needs and desires; however, you will become more self-aware, confident, and comfortable with confrontations. The meditation poses commonly practiced to activate it include: root lock, front stretches, lying on the stomach, chain pose, crow pose, frog pose, front stretches, and body drops.

Overview of the root chakra:

- Focus: survival, security, self-acceptance and the power of habit.
- Location: the base of the spinal cord, between sex organs and the anal sphincter.
- Organ: colon, the organ of elimination.
- Element: earth.
- Color: red.
- Asanas: crow pose, root lock, front stretches, chair pose, lying on the stomach, frog pose, and body drops.

7.2 Swadhisthana, the Sacral Chakra

This chakra is associated with our sensual needs and desires such as sexual energy and reproduction. As a matter of fact, it is located near the sex organs. The activation of this chakra enables us to experience our sensual side and recognize our inner desires and strengths. This is a state of self-recognition and awareness. Practicing meditations focused on the sacral chakra helps us experience and control the flow of sexual desires and energy. The organs associated with this chakra are sex organs such as uterus, ovaries, vagina, fallopian tubes, kidneys, adrenal glands, and bladder for women, and penis, scrotum, bladder, adrenal glands, and kidneys for men. Since it's associated with the power of sensual energy, its element is water.

Asanas that help activate it are: sat kriya, frog pose, pelvic lifts, cat-cow pose, cobra pose, and butterfly pose.

Overview on the sacral chakra:

- Focus: sexual desire, sexual energy, and reproduction.
- Location: sexual organs.
- Organ: sexual organs and glands.
- Element: water.
- Color: orange.
- Asanas: frog pose, butterfly pose, sat kriya, cobra pose, cat-cow pose, and pelvic lifts.

7.3 Manipura, the Solar Plexus Chakra

This chakra is located in the navel area, which is known as the solar plexus and is the center of action. We often find ourselves unable to do something to achieve our life goals. When we feel like this, our navel chakra is most probably blocked, which makes us feel frustrated and angry.

If it's activated, this chakra canalizes your energy and power and neutralizes negative energy. As a result, we can focus more on our life goals.

Apart from the willpower and canalizing of physical strength, this chakra is associated with the digestive system. Proper regulation of digestive organs is regulated by practicing meditations focused on the naval chakra.

Asanas associated with the third chakra are: diaphragm lock, fire breathing, sat kriya, stretch pose, and the bow pose.

Overview of the solar plexus chakra:

- Focus: action, individual strength, balance, and commitment.
- Location: solar plexus and navel region.
- Organ: pancreas, stomach, small intestine, liver, solar plexus, pancreas, gall bladder, spleen, and large intestine.
- Element: fire.
- Color: yellow.
- Asanas: breath of fire, stretch pose, sat kriya, diaphragm lock, and bow pose.

7.4 Anahata, the heart chakra

Anahata chakra is the center point of the upper and lower triangle chakras and corresponds to the location of the soul. It is located in the center of the chest and near the heart, which is associated with strong feelings and radiates compassion, passion, love, and other strong feelings but also loneliness, disappointment, despair, and helplessness. It connects physical energy and emotions to the divinity. Now, the main goal is to trigger the feelings of compassion, trust, divinity, and unity through this energy center. Meditations and kriyas associated with the heart chakra must be practiced regularly and consistently to achieve the highest levels of self-awareness and consciousness.

Meditations and poses that stimulate this energy center include: all arm poses, ego eradicator, yoga mudra, pranayama, and baby pose.

Overview of the heart chakra:
- Focus: selfless service, awakening of spiritual awareness, ability to let go, and connection with divinity.

- Location: in the center of the chest.
- Organ: lungs, heart, and thymus gland.
- Element: air.
- Color: green.
- Asanas: baby pose, yoga mudra, pranayama, and ego eradicator.

7.5 Vishuddha, the Throat Chakra

This chakra is associated with the power to speak and listen. The metabolic reactions controlled by the thyroid gland are associated with the throat chakra as well. It focuses on the connection and conversation with your inner self and the divinity on a more spiritual level. The stimulation of this chakra will make you understand the real truth of the world and the divinity and will help you navigate between the real and divine world. Organs associated with this chakra are the throat, trachea, and backbone at the cervical vertebra level.

Overview of the throat chakra:

- Focus: real truth, connection to the divine force, speak and listen to the truth, understand the true meaning of life.

- Location: in the center of the throat.
- Organ: throat, cervical vertebra, thyroid gland, and trachea.
- Element: ether.
- Color: light blue.
- Asanas: cat-cow, chants, plow pose, neck lock, and cobra pose.

7.6 Ajna, third eye chakra

This chakra is also known as the third eye chakra and is very important because it represents the union between body and mind. It is located is at the pituitary gland, which is in the center of the forehead above eyebrows. As a matter of fact, it's the point where two different energies meet (Pingala and Ida). Focusing on meditations directed towards the third eye will help you achieve the highest level of consciousness and find your inner self. Focusing on the third eye helps stimulate the power of intuition and gain confidence, wisdom, and self-awareness; this is the last step towards reaching divinity. In doing so, you can totally control both your mind and your body. When the relaxed consciousness reaches its highest level, you experience a higher level of consciousness and self-awareness.

Useful asanas include archer pose, resting the forehead on the floor, and all the exercises related to the resting forehead. In order to strengthen this chakra, you should breathe through alternate nostrils or practice the kirtan kriya.

Overview of the third eye chakra:

- Focus: identity, wisdom, and intuition.
- Location: above the eyebrows and in the center of the forehead (pituitary gland).
- Organ: brain and pituitary gland.
- Element: not specified.
- Color: indigo.
- Asanas: breathing with alternate nostril, focusing on the third eye location, whistle breathing, archer pose, resting the forehead on the floor, and kirtan kriya.

7.7 Sahasrara, the Crown Chakra

The crown chakra is associated with the path or the gateway to enlightenment. It is located at the crown of the head and is associated with the brain and the perineal gland. The crown chakra represents the ultimate goal, which is achieving enlightenment. This chakra is considered the highest point or the location of the soul and helps get in touch with the divinity.

Overview of the crown chakra:

- Focus: purpose of life, inner peace, and divinity.
- Location: at the top of the head
- Organ: brain and perineal gland.
- Element: not specified.
- Color: violet.
- Asanas: sat kriya, focus on the nose, and ego eradicator.

Understanding how chakras work will help you in your journey towards enlightenment and will make your kundalini yoga practice more effective.

Chapter 8
Kundalini Awakening

In this chapter, we will discuss the meaning and the experience of kundalini awakening. As it was mentioned in the previous chapters, kundalini is represented by the feminine energy placed at the base part of the spinal cord. The main goal of kundalini yoga is to activate that sleeping energy, allowing it to flow throughout the body and the seven chakras. As a result, you will feel positive both physically and mentally.

Kundalini awakening is associated with enlightenment and gaining the highest level of consciousness. In order to do so, the feminine energy has to uncoil, move through the seven chakras, and reach the crown chakra, which is associated with consciousness, intuition, and the connection between the physical body and the divinity. When the feminine energy connects to the masculine energy, kundalini awakening reaches its highest point.

How would you know how you feel during the kundalini awakening? This is a rather difficult question because each person experiences it differently. However, it can be said that you might feel a great amount of energy rushing into your body. You may also feel overwhelmed and not be able to understand what's happening.

At this point, you could ask another question; will everyone who practices yoga be able to experience a kundalini awakening? It may sound disappointing, but the truth is kundalini awakening is rare. Sometimes it is achieved after practicing for many years, while other people might experience it quite spontaneously. While some people who have been practicing yoga and meditation for a long time just can't experience it, other people who aren't even trying might achieve it without any effort. However, there is more than one way to experience a kundalini awakening. Sometimes even emotional, mental, or physical trauma can activate and uncoil the kundalini shakti. This spontaneous awakening can occur at any time.

In brief, kundalini awakening might be experienced:

1. After many years of meditation and practice
2. Quite spontaneously.

- Directed Awakening:

Yogis and gurus who practice kundalini yoga make a great effort to reach the enlightenment; however, they might never experience any sort of kundalini awakening. Even though you might feel discouraged, you have to remember that the experience of yoga itself is worth it. Moreover, kundalini awakening has something to do with Karma. According to Hindu mythology, the physical body is only a vessel for the soul, which never dies and just changes its shape. Therefore, your previous Karma has a strong impact on your current life and on kundalini awakening. In general, don't feel discouraged. Here are some advice from teachers and gurus who claimed they have experienced a kundalini awakening:

1. Meditations:

Meditating in a calm and peaceful place could be the key to experience a kundalini awakening. As a matter of fact, you might have heard of some yoga students and gurus who spend some time in the Himalayas. They do this to stimulate the feminine shakti.

However, you should always remember what was said before; some people could experience a kundalini awakening quite spontaneously. Unfortunately, there are no hard-and-fast rules to reach this point. In other words, experiencing an awakening is like getting a PhD in kundalini yoga. However, unlike traditional degrees, there's no way you can make sure that all the effort you put into it will be rewarded. This is a self-regulatory occurrence, and there is no way to control it.

2. Asanas

Some asanas are directed towards kundalini awakenings. They are known to stimulate and activate the chakras. By practicing these postures consistently and using mantras that align with the energy and the vibrations of the body, you can trigger a kundalini awakening. Apart from kundalini and hatha yoga, tai chi and qi gong could also help you in doing so.

3. Breathing Routine:

Kundalini breathing exercises are called Pranayama. If you practice them correctly and consistently, you could trigger the awakening. As a matter of fact, while you are in control of your breath and you guide it to the energy centers located in your body, you stimulate the crown chakra. Now, it takes a lot of time and practice, but it could also be very helpful if you would like to experience a kundalini awakening.

4. Praying:

Intentions have a strong impact on your body and its reactions. Similarly, if you practice yoga with devotion and dedication, you'll have better chances of reaching the enlightenment.

- Spontaneous Awakening:

When you experience a spontaneous awakening, you achieve a higher level of consciousness without even trying. Below there are some circumstances where awakenings have occurred:

1. Healing Processes:

People often need assistance to heal themselves from trauma. Sometimes they seek refuge in yoga or reiki, or go through therapy; meanwhile, they could experience something like a kundalini awakening. As a matter of fact, energy centers are unknowingly unblocked, and there is a free flow of kundalini shakti, which may lead to a kundalini awakening.

2. Treatment of Physical Trauma:

We know that the coiled Kundalini is located at the base of the spinal cord. If you accidentally injure your lower back, you will focus on this part while healing, which may sometimes trigger a kundalini awakening.

3. Childbirth:

Childbirth is the biggest miracle in life. There is a small creature breathing and growing within the womb, which is where the root chakra is located. During childbirth, there is a lot of physical energy involved, which may trigger a kundalini awakening in the mother.

4. Falling in Love:

According to scientific research, when we fall in love, oxytocin is released in our bodies, making us experience love and belonging. However, what causes the oxytocin to release, and how is it released?

Falling in love means experiencing a strong energy flow, and it can also activate the heart chakra. As a result, a kundalini awakening may occur.

5. Emotional Trauma:

Going through an emotional trauma like the death of a close family member or friend can also trigger the intense flow of energy throughout the body. Any trigger can activate the chakras, and it does not necessarily have to be a positive trigger. Sometimes stress and depression create a rush of emotion, and the body goes on to experience a kundalini awakening because it is going through a lot of emotional pain and suffering.

6. An Almost Fatal Experience:

When you lie between life and death, all mental and physical energies converge towards a certain point to save your life. As a result, you may experience a kundalini awakening.

8.1 How Safe is Kundalini Awakening?

Kundalini awakening is a shift of energy and an energy rush that can sometimes be overwhelming for those who are not prepared enough. What happens when you experience a kundalini awakening is that the ego in your physical body breaks down, and you can see the truth. The feminine power is a positive, pure, and nurturing energy, but a sudden rush of energy can sometimes be an overwhelming experience for someone who is not fully prepared for it. Kundalini awakening sometimes makes you conscious of the greater truth, and absorbing and sustaining that sort of vision after living most of your life less consciously can be frightening for some people. Practicing meditations and kriyas to bring about a kundalini awakening is safe. However, it is always recommended to talk to a guru who can guide you throughout this great transition. After experiencing a kundalini awakening, you should strengthen and purify your whole body and mind to endure and sustain this new state of consciousness.

You should never rush the awakening; it should be gradual, and your body and mind should be prepared for such a change. Moreover, you should always have a teacher on your side who can help you benefit from the awakening.

8.2 Signs and Symptoms of Kundalini Awakening

As it was previously explained, kundalini awakening is always a different and unique experience for each one of us. Now we will discuss what you might experience when the awakening occurs:

- Sudden changes in the physical body. You may experience

cold sweats, fever, and body shivering. Some people may also experience extreme chilliness in the body, followed by hot flashes. These are some of the most common symptoms of a kundalini awakening.

- You may become overwhelmed with a sudden rush of emotions. You may experience sudden outbursts of crying or extreme restlessness, and a tingling or an itching sensation at the level of your spinal cord.
- You may experience physical stress, and you might feel that there is huge energy or a huge weight on your chest.
- You might become emotionally overburdened. This new sense of truth, the disappearance of the veil of your physical ego, and the appearance of clarity and truth will make you overwhelmed. You might feel depressed and disconnected from your previous self.
- Another thing you may experience is clear dreams. These will be raw and real dreams, and you will be unable to distinguish them from reality.
- You will feel disconnected from the physical world around you. You will be able to see things from a greater perspective, and it will become awkward and uncomfortable for you to associate yourself with the physical world you've always known.
- You will be able to say the truth with confidence and clarity because the throat chakra has been activated. People will perceive your behavior as unusual because what you are saying is now based on truth, and you don't want to please other people around you.
- Gradually, you will be able to feel well in your physical body. Kundalini awakening also releases energy within the body, which can be healed as a result. You feel physical strength and a stronger immune system. Moreover, your body can endure a large spectrum of physical conditions without being affected.
- You will experience an urge for selfless service; you will feel empathy for people and find yourself taking part in activities that encourage service to mankind.

- Your mind will become clear, and you will look at things from a positive perspective. You will not see things and situations in a way that affects you, and you will start looking at the big picture, wishing to make the world a better place to live. You will feel that positivity, forgiveness, and empathy have taken over your body.
- Your spirituality will peak, and you will find yourself in a deep relationship with divinity, while feeling cut off from the world.
- Your mind will slowly become void of judgment. You will not look at things negatively and will use your intuition and inner energy to understand and summarize situations.
- Your focus will now be on the big picture. Normally, before doing something, people think at what advantages this type of activity will provide them. On the other hand, you will not think only about yourself, but about the big picture, that is how your actions will positively affect others and what needs to be done.
- You will find that your body and mind are calm and in balance.
- You will feel this urge from within that encourages you to change. You will share how yoga has affected you and want to try to help people live a better life.
- You will find yourself promoting peace and stopping taking part in anything that includes violence.

8.3 What Can You Do to Experience Kundalini Awakening?

In this part, we will discuss asanas, hand movements, and other things that play a big role in kundalini yoga.

- Breathing exercises:

It is well known that breathing exercises are beneficial for the human body if done properly. Apart from that, they help you with the regulation of body processes and can also trigger a kundalini awakening.

- Asanas

Asanas are postures you hold for a long time. It is believed that some of them can help release kundalini energy. Many yogis practice the following asanas when they are trying to experience a kundalini awakening.

1. Sat Kriya

This asana focuses on the crown chakra. Just sit down on your knees and stretch your back while performing a neck lock with your head and neck. Pull up your chest and navel, then raise your hands and arms above the head, which must be in between your elbows. Your arms must be straight, while your hands are pressed against each other. Now join your pinky, ring, and middle fingers, while pointing both index fingers towards the sky and joining thumbs. For women, the left hand's thumb should be on top of the right hand, while for men it's the opposite. This posture is known as the sat kriya and is the most powerful posture of kundalini yoga.

2. Malasana

This is also good for beginners and is directed towards the sacral and the root chakra. The organs associated with this asana are the spleen and the stomach. First, keep your legs apart equal to the width of your shoulders and sit down in a squatting position while doing the neck lock. Your back must be straight, your navel is slightly pulled towards it, and your hands are in the prayer position. This asana is also known as the garland asana and activates kundalini energy, directing it from the root to the sacral chakra. This asana really helps the digestive system. As a matter of fact, it is believed that the activation of energy within this area of the body facilitates proper digestion and elimination of toxins. Overall, it brings positivity and helps get rid of negative energy.

3. Balasana

"Bal" means "child" in Sanskrit, and this asana is also known as the child pose because it mimics the position of a baby in the mother's womb. This asana, which can also be performed by beginners, is focused on relaxing and is practiced by many yogis after a stressful and difficult kriya. If performed for one to three minutes, it has many benefits for both body and mind because it refreshes and resets energy. Moreover, it helps relieve stress and strengthens the muscles. As a result, the body is connected to its origin, the starting point of life.

Join your knees and sit down on them. Your hips must be on your feet, which are joined as well. Now place your arms on your hips and slowly bend, while touching the floor or the yoga mat with your forehead. Your arms must be relaxed and pointed towards the feet. Hold this position for one to three minutes. It calms the nerves, improves blood circulation, and helps unlock energy blockages within the spinal cord, shoulders, and neck. Moreover, this asana is known to help the digestive system.

4. Dhanurasana

This asana is also known as the bow pose, works well for losing weight, and helps release stress. It opens up the heart and purifies feelings, making it easier to accept the truth and dissolve the ego. This pose is difficult to hold but has many advantages. Specifically, it helps the reproductive organs, making them stronger and more toned. Moreover, it's known to facilitate the production of insulin, making it easier to lose weight and activate the metabolism.

This asana is particularly focused on the solar plexus chakra. While practicing it, you will probably feel like your solar plexus is tightening up. First, lie down on your stomach and lay your arms on the side of your body. Then hold your legs apart equal to the width of your hips, lift them up, and bend your knees so that they move closer to the buttocks. Now use your hands to hold your feet at the mid-point and move them away from the buttocks. As a result, your torso will lift from the ground, and your heart will open up. Hold your neck straight and your chin high. Hold the position for 30 seconds and then relax laying down on your stomach for 30 to 60 seconds. After that, perform the asana again.

5. Mandukasana

This difficult asana is also known as the frog pose, helps with posture and relieve stress and back and hip pain. It directly targets the body's core and opens up hips and the groin area. If you are a beginner, do not perform this asana and first focus on improving your flexibility.

This asana is performed by setting yourself in a tabletop position or another position where you are balancing on your four limbs. Place your arms below the shoulders and your knees below the hips. Now open up your knees as far as possible. Then move your feet outwards by flexing your ankles so that the inner parts of your feet move near the floor. Listen to your body and stop if you can't handle moving forward. Remember not to overstretch your body. At this point, take a deep breath and release. Bend your body and spread your arms straight on the floor with your palms down. Hold the position for 30 seconds and then get back to the tabletop position.

6. Ustrasana

This asana is also known as the camel pose or the backbend. It helps with back problems and pain in the lower part of the back.

Sit down on your knees and keep them aligned with your hips. Now distance your knees, open your shoulders, bend backward, and touch your feet with your fingers. As a result, your back will be stretched. Now move your head backward and try to focus on your nose.

7. Bhujangasana:

This asana is also known as the cobra pose and is connected to the throat chakra. This pose is good for the back and spinal cord flexibility.

Lay down on your stomach and bend your arms under your shoulders. Move your legs slightly apart, push your hands to the ground, and lay your feet on the ground while pointing the toes backward. Now stretch your arms, while pushing with them on the ground and lifting your upper torso. The lower torso should remain rested on the ground. Move your chin upward and your head towards the back while stretching your arms. Hold this position for 30 seconds to one minute and then get back to the ground. After a 15-second rest, perform the asana again.

Mantras

We know that mantras stimulate vibrations, thus bringing about the energy shift. As follows, you can find chants that stimulate the energy flow within the body.

1. LAM

This chant is most effective when repeated, while performing kriyas and meditations directed towards the root chakra. Along with specific kriyas, it stimulates the unblocking and release of energy from it.

2. VAM

This chant is most effective when repeated, while performing kriyas and meditations directed towards the sacral chakra. Along with specific kriyas, it stimulates the unblocking and release of energy from it.

3. RAM

This chant is most effective when repeated, while performing kriyas and meditations directed towards the solar plexus chakra. Along with specific kriyas, it stimulates the unblocking and release of energy from it.

4. YAM

This chant is most effective when repeated, while performing kriyas and meditations directed towards the solar plexus chakra. Along with the specific kriyas, it helps with the unblocking and release of energy from it.

5. HAM

This chant is most effective when repeated, while performing kriyas and meditations directed towards the throat chakra. Along with specific kriyas, it helps with the unblocking and release of energy from it.

6. AUM

This chant is most effective when repeated, while performing kriyas and meditations directed towards the third eye chakra. Along with specific kriyas, it stimulates the unblocking and release of energy from it.

7. Silence

Silent concentration is practiced, while performing meditations and kriyas directed towards the crown chakra.

- Mudras

Mudras are specific hand movements and postures practiced during yoga. As follows, you can find some mudras that could help you trigger kundalini awakening:

1. The thousand petals mudra

This mudra is performed, while focusing on the crown chakra. Just stretch your arms above your head, open both your hands, and join the thumb and index fingertips together.

2. The great head mudra:

This mudra, which is also known as Mahasirs mudra, could help you heal headaches and sinus problems. While sitting down comfortably, put your hands with palms upward. Then join the tips of your thumbs, index fingers, and middle fingers, and face the hands upwards. Now curl the ring finger into the palm of your hand, while keeping the pinky finger stretched and holding this position for six minutes.

3. Granthi Mudra:

The Granthi mudra, which is also known as the knot mudra, is used to activate the throat chakra and is associated with self-healing. It balances your throat chakra and thyroid glands. It is often used for people who suffer from cancer to make them feel relieved, safe, and in balance. By activating the throat chakra, this mudra also affects the way you speak, making you sound calm and clear. Therefore, it also improves your confidence.

Sit down with your back stretched and hold both your hands in front of you. Remember that your head must be in the neck lock position. Now interlace your fingers and hold the right-hand thumb, touching the tip of left-hand index finger; the left-hand thumb must touch the right-hand index finger. Then hold both of your hands forward near the throat. Hold this position for five to ten minutes, while doing specific breathing exercises.

4. Muladhara Mudra

This mudra is associated with the root chakra and helps activate organs and energies associated with it. Sit down with your legs crossed and hold your hands in prayer position. Then stretch your back and neck and perform a neck lock.

Now interlace your pinky and ring fingers. Keep your middle fingers pressed against each other and hold them upright. Now interlace your index fingers and thumbs so that they form two loops. Turn both the hands in the same position downwards, pointing to the pelvis.

5. The Shakti Mudra:

This mudra is associated with the sacral chakra and is known to control sexual desires and help keep sensuality in balance.

This mudra is performed by holding the hands in the prayer position and then pressing the pinky fingers and ring fingers against each other, keeping them upright. Then fold your thumbs into the palms and your index and middle fingers over them so that thumbs are locked within the fingers. Now push the index- and middle-finger knuckles together. Hold the lower parts of the hands pressed just below the navel.

6. The Rudra Mudra:

This mudra is associated with the solar plexus chakra and with the Hindu god Vishnu. Practicing this mudra brings about self-control inside your mind and body and improves your confidence.

Sit down in a relaxed position and put your hands with the palms up on both your thighs. Now join your indexes and ring fingers at the tip of the thumb.

7. The Padma Mudra:

This mudra is associated with the heart chakra. It resembles a blossoming flower. Hold the lower parts of your palms together and press them together with your thumbs and pinky fingers. This mudra opens up your heart to new possibilities, new beginnings, and happiness, making you feel more empathetic and able to look at the big picture.

Chapter 9
Psychic Ability Through Yoga

This chapter will discuss how to develop psychic abilities through yoga and meditation. According to some people, this is a far-fetched concept. We actually live in a world where believing is equal to seeing, and such abilities are considered unusual and sometimes also supernatural. However, in this chapter, we will discuss meditations and techniques to develop psychic abilities.

Psychic ability is like knowing about the unknown, and the third eye chakra deals with such energies. You can't see these kind of energies, but there're here, guiding you towards consciousness. Actually, every type of yoga and meditation will help you develop psychic abilities because yoga aligns your internal energies with the outside world. Over time, your heart and mind will open up to consciousness, and you will develop some sort of psychic abilities.

Below you can find the most effective meditations to bring about psychic intuition and abilities:

9.1 Ajna Dhyana Meditation

This type of meditation is very ancient and has been practiced for thousands of years. It is focused on the third eye chakra and on making energies flow through it.

As follows, you can find instructions to perform this meditation:

- Sit down in a relaxed position.
- Put your head in the neck lock position.

- Put your hands on your knees and slowly join your indexes and middle fingers tips together.
- Without moving your head, focus on the third eye spot between the eyebrows and visualize it.
- Use the chant OM while inhaling deeply.
- Continue for five minutes.
- Close your eyes and focus on the third eye.
- Chant OM while breathing deeply.
- Continue for five minutes.
- Gradually open your eyes, focus on your forehead, and breathe deeply for one minute.

9.2 Samyama Meditation

In order to perform this meditation, you have to focus your energies on someone or something specific. As a matter of fact, this is sort of a directed meditation.

For this meditation, follow these steps:

- Keep a picture of the person or the thing you chose beside you.
- Sit in a relaxed position and keep your back stretched.
- Close your eyes and place your hands on your lap.
- Start breathing deeply, do 108 breaths, and concentrate on the person or the thing portrayed in the photo.
- Open your eyes, take the picture and focus on it with breathing 108 times, or until you feel that you are connected to this person or thing.
- While breathing, if you feel any insights, acknowledge them, and let them flow.
- Close your eyes and see yourself connected to the person or thing you chose.
- Breathe 108 times and feel any insights you perceive. This is psychic knowledge, and the vision you see, or feel is intuition.
- Feel the intuition and let it flow through your body.

- Meditate for 20 minutes, and then open your eyes. Thank the supreme power or energy for the insights.
- You can practice this every day to develop your psychic abilities.

Mantra for Psychic Abilities

This is the most effective mantra to develop psychic abilities: OM HAM NAMO DEYAVA.

Repeat this mantra 108 times in the morning, afternoon, and at night.

Chapter 10

Postures for the Nervous System

We know that our nervous system controls our actions and emotions. You need a strong nervous system to live a balanced and effective life. In this chapter, we will discuss some postures and asanas that are beneficial for the nervous system. When performed over time, these postures will strengthen it effectively.

10.1 Balasana

This asana is also known as the child pose and stimulates the digestive system as well as the nervous system.

Instructions

Sit down on your heels and gradually move forward, while bending your back and stretching your arms. Bend until your head touches the ground, and your arms are fully stretched forward. If you perform this asana for two minutes every morning, it will neutralize your positive and negative energy and provide balance to the nervous system. Therefore, it is effective for people who suffer from anxiety and low self-esteem.

Generally, you should perform Balasana every day. However, if you feel anxious and restless, you can repeat it one more time. As a result, your blood will be directed towards your brain and will stimulate it. By putting your head on the ground, you cancel other electromagnetic fields and both positive and negative energy around you. As a result, when you get up, you will feel renewed and ready to take on the day. You can also perform Balasana before an important meeting for an excellent performance. Moreover, this asana is very beneficial for the spine and gives it a great stretch, stimulating the energy flow through it.

10.2 Halasana

This difficult asana is also known as the plow pose and is highly effective for stimulating the nervous system and also clearing the sinuses. While practicing it, a lot of blood is provided to the brain, stimulating and recharging it.

Instructions

Since this asana is really difficult, you shouldn't perform it until you become flexible enough. You should first master easier asanas and meditations before trying this out. However, if you're not a beginner, follow these instructions. Lay down on the yoga mat and put your arms on the side of your torso. Now lift both your legs and move them upwards over the stomach, while banding your head. Then take your legs back until they reach the ground, and you are in a curved position.

If you are dealing with high blood pressure, diabetes, or asthma, you should talk to your doctor before trying out new asanas. Remember that it all depends on your body's needs and never try to do something that could put your body in danger.

10.3 Ardha Matsyendrasana

This asana is also known as the spinal twist yoga pose and stimulates clearing and detoxification. Moreover, it regulates the nervous and immune system. Detoxification and cleansing processes of the body are particularly helpful for the nervous system, which is reenergized. This asana helps with concentration and stimulates the areas of the brain that manage multitasking. You should definitely try this asana if you have a busy schedule or manage multiple tasks at once.

Instructions

Move your right leg over your left thigh and place the right foot on the floor. Then push the left foot back so that it touches the hip. Now place the right hand on the floor and the palm downward. Place the left arm elbow on the knee and hold the position for one to three minutes.

This yoga pose should be performed at least once a day because it helps get rid of toxins. Performing this pose for three minutes every day for one week will also help with mental clarity and agility; you will feel that emotional stamina and mental ability are positively affected by including this posture in your yoga routine.

However, you should always stop if the stretching is too much, and you don't feel flexible enough. Give your body time and space to grow and become more familiar with this. Yoga is one of the safest activities and exercises to do, but you are responsible for your own body. So, keep track of what you can do and do not push beyond your limits. This asana is not as easy as it looks in the picture, and the first time you try it out you will probably feel a deep stretch in your back. While practicing yoga, the most important thing is to become aware of how far you can go; try to push yourself beyond your limits but stop if you realize you can't do it safely. The key is to be patient and consistent.

10.4 Anuloma Viloma

This asana is also known as the alternate breathing asana and is beneficial for the brain because it stimulates the nervous system. Moreover, it helps open sinuses and with your lungs.

Instructions

Sit down and place your right hand on your left nostril, while breathing deeply through the right nostril. Now hold your breath and place your hand on the right nostril to block it, while exhaling through the left nostril. Breathe alternately through your right and left nostrils for 5 minutes. Apart from brain strength and toning to the nervous system, this asana is helpful for the respiratory system as well. By doing this asana, you improve your control over your mind and learn how to let go of all negativities in your body. Most of neurodegenerative diseases can be prevented and controlled by regularly practicing this asana. It is also useful to prevent diseases like diabetes, cholesterol, and hypertension and has a positive effect on your overall mood.

10.5 Adho Mukha Svanasana

This asana is also known as the downward dog pose and stimulates the nervous system as well as the immune system. Performing this asana can increase the production of white blood cells in the body.

Instructions

Find your way to the table pose, gradually lift your torso, and force your hips to move higher by moving a bit forward. Hold this portion for 10 to 15 seconds.

This is excellent to tone and activate the immune system, which is controlled by the lymphatic system. As a matter of fact, this asana helps with the lymphatic drainage.

Chapter 11
Postures for Sexual Abilities

One of the most interesting things about yoga is how it affect sexuality. Nowadays, we are really stressed and find it difficult to keep our lives in balance. As a result, intimate relationships may have a hard time. However, practicing yoga can help you with your sexual health. In this chapter, you can find a few postures that affect your sexual abilities.

11.1 Reclined Cobbler's Pose

To perform this pose, follow these steps:

- Lay down on the floor or on a yoga mat.
- Stretch your arms and put them on the side of your torso.
- Join the lower side of both your feet and hold this position.
- Stretch your hands outwards at about 45 degrees angle on both sides.
- Practice deep breathing with your eyes closed.
- Hold the pose for 10 minutes, while focusing on root chakra.
- Keep your mind as free as possible.

The reclined cobbler's pose, which is also known as the Supta Baddha Konasana, opens up your pelvic bone and makes your sexual organs flexible. Your overall sexual health will benefit from it. Sometimes, stress causes a lower libido, frustration, and anxiety. However, the reclined cobbler's pose helps open up the root chakra and also triggers the release of oxytocin in the blood, which improves the libido.

11.2 Downward Dog Pose

This is also an effective pose to control your sexual energies. Just follow these instructions to practice it:

- Stand straight and open your feet apart around the width of your shoulders.
- With your head down, start bending your back towards the front, reaching for the floor, and resting your arms on the ground.
- Keep your body arched.
- Squeeze your navel.
- Hold the posture for 30 seconds if you are a beginner.
- With time and practice, increase the duration.

The head downwards allows the blood to flow towards the brain and stimulates the release of adrenalin and oxytocin, which helps your sexual abilities. The arch shape provides flexibility to the backbone and the pelvic muscles, which is also beneficial for the libido.

11.3 Cat and Cow Pose

While practicing this meditation, you actually alternate between two poses. This pose, which is also known as Marjariasana-Bitilasana, will strengthen your core and your sexual organs, bringing flexibility to your spinal cord. As follows, you can find instructions to perform the cat and cow pose:

- Find your way to a table pose on your yoga mat.
- While inhaling, drop your head and bend your spine, stretching it as high as possible.
- While exhaling, arch your back downward with your hip sticking outward, hold your head high, and try to stretch your neck, while pushing the chin forward.
- Repeat it six times and keep breathing.

The cat and cow pose provides flexibility to the backbone, the pectoral muscles, and the pelvic area. As a matter of fact, it stimulates the secretion of oxytocin, which provides tone to the pectoral and pelvic muscles. This yoga pose is also beneficial for people who are trying to conceive a baby because it tones the uterine muscles and facilitates egg implantation.

11.4 Bridge Pose

This pose is also known as the Setubandha pose. It opens up your chest and encourages openness, acceptability, and compatibility, which positively affect sexuality.

This is recommended for beginners and obese people. As follows, you can find instructions to perform this pose:

- Lie down on the mat.
- Put your arms facing down near your torso.
- Bend your legs and place your feet on the mat as if you were trying to stand up.
- Push your feet down and try to lift your thighs and hips.
- With thighs lifted and parallel to the floor, hold the position for 30 seconds.

This pose increases libido and strengthens the pelvic and pectoral muscles. It also tones up the hip opening and the spine, which also helps sexuality and flexibility.

Apart from sexual abilities, this posture is also very effective for stress and anxiety. If you practice it for one month, it helps you get rid of migraines and also improves your overall mood and confidence.

11.5 11.6. Chair Pose

This pose is also known as the Utkata pose and strengthens the core, which is where all sexual organs are located. Moreover, it tones the muscles and provides them with flexibility as well. To perform the chair pose, follow these instructions:

- Stand the mountain pose on the yoga mat.
- Move your body as if you were sitting on an imaginary chair.

- Hold the pose for 30 seconds.

This pose triggers the root chakra and the secretion of adrenalin and oxytocin. Therefore, it is beneficial for keeping the right and left sides of the brain in balance. If you practice it every day for two months, it will help control high blood pressure, and you will notice lowering in overall values. Moreover, this pose helps with lower back and lower abdomen pain and with weight loss.

Chapter 12
The Health and Wellness Benefits of Yoga

Yoga helps you keep physically and mentally healthy, gain spiritual knowledge, and live peacefully. If you practice it regularly, you might already know its numerous benefits. As a matter of fact, yoga has been gaining attention worldwide, and International Yoga Day is celebrated on June 21st. Now let's discuss its benefits in detail.

12.1 Why Should We Practice Yoga?

You should practice yoga to live healthy both physically and mentally, to be positive, and to reflect on yourself. In this chapter, we have tried to gather the main benefits of yoga on everyday life:

- It helps you physically, mentally, and spiritually in many ways.
- It helps you be healthy.
- It helps your mental development.
- It increases intelligence and sharpness.
- It gets rid of anxiety and stress.
- It brings positivity and gets rid of negative energy.
- It provides agility and vigor and makes your body and your muscles more flexible.
- It helps you avoid suffering from many diseases.
- It brings peace to your mind.
- It helps you concentrate.
- It helps with obesity.

- It makes you more beautiful.
- It increases self-confidence.
- It improves blood flow.
- It improves flexibility of the muscles and helps the digestive system.
- It helps you keep your body, mind, brain, and spirit in balance.
- It treats many diseases.
- It helps in driving away from laziness.
- It increases your energy level.
- It increases stamina.
- It brings you inner peace.

Many diseases can be controlled and sometimes cured by practicing yoga (e.g., physical injuries, high blood pressure, diabetes, arthritis etc.). Unlike other workouts, the main goal of yoga is overall health. Moreover, asanas are focused on target areas and can be tailored to one's needs. This is why yoga is so amazing.

12.2 Diabetes

If you practice yoga regularly, you can keep diabetes under control because it stimulates the production of insulin.

Some yoga exercises and asanas that are focused on the sacral chakra to trigger the production of insulin in the body, which lowers the sugar level in the blood and gets rid of fat deposits. As a result, you may also lose some weight.

A lot of people worldwide already suffer from type 2 diabetes, but the thing is they are also increasing with time. A large cut of the American population is affected by diabetes, especially young people. Previously, diabetes was believed not to be treatable at all; it was considered as a lifelong disease that could only be controlled through medication. Nowadays, it is widely known that diabetes can be managed thanks to adequate food and physical exercise. Yoga can help people who suffer from diabetes to get off medication and lead a normal life.

12.3 Hypertension

High blood pressure is also on the rise, and now young people suffer from it as well. Previously, high blood pressure was believed to only affect people over the age of 50; now there are people in their late twenties and early thirties suffering from it. This is alarming because getting it diagnosed at an early age also means that you will probably risk heart diseases in the future.

Most of the time, high blood pressure is related to stress. It is widely acknowledged that we live in a very stressful world, work in highly competitive environments, and struggle with balancing work and free time. In such conditions, if we take out some time to practice yoga, we will benefit from it in terms of keeping our high blood sugar level under control. As a matter of fact, it can be lowered by doing calming exercises and practicing deep breathing to regulate the heart rate and tone the heat muscle. If you wish a healthier heart and a longer life for yourself, start doing yoga now. Begin with easy exercises and then challenge yourself with more difficult asanas and meditations.

12.4 Cholesterol

Cholesterol is the accumulation of fat inside arteries, which makes the circulatory system work less effectively. Yoga also helps with clearing arteries, and postures focused on the heart chakra are work well to the control cholesterol. Including yoga in your routine can help you control and lower the cholesterol level in the blood. However, cholesterol cannot be controlled by just doing yoga; you also need to work on your lifestyle and diet to bring about a drastic change. The sooner you take charge of your health, the sooner you can get rid of this big problem.

12.5 Mental Health

The main goal of yoga is to achieve overall wellness. It's not just a matter of physical wellness but of mental health as well. Research has proven the positive effects yoga has on mental health.

Yoga is primarily useful for people who suffer from anxiety and depression. For mild cases, yoga alone is enough to treat the condition and instill a feeling of wellness in students. Yoga is known to prevent or delay the onset of many neurodegenerative diseases such as Alzheimer's, dementia, and Parkinson's disease.

Mental health is not taken seriously enough in our society, but there is research claiming that one third of the world population have suffered from some sort of mental health issues in their life. Therefore, it's necessary to prevent this from happening. By practicing yoga, you can improve your mental health and your quality of life. Start early so that you won't have any regrets later in life.

12.6 Skin and Hair

Practicing yoga has anti-ageing effects on the body. For example, it prevents white hair from appearing at an early age. Apart from this, your hair will shine if you practice yoga regularly. Moreover, your blood circulation will improve, allowing your hair follicles to be more nourished; as a result, your hair will grow stronger and healthier. Similarly, practicing yoga has a positive effect on the skin because it prevents wrinkles from appearing too early in life. Since blood circulation is improved, the body cells are nourished, and this has visible effects on skin, hair, and nails. Your skin will feel softer and more supple. These positive effects on skin and hair make people think that yoga makes you beautiful; however, it is just a matter of health and nourishment.

Nowadays, people are very stressed and don't have much time

for themselves. It is widely acknowledged that stress causes hair loss and skin problems. Hair and skin products have positive effects for some time, but they are not very helpful in the long run. On the other hand, yoga provides you with better skin and hair. This is because it stimulates healing to happen from within; as a matter of fact, it deals with keeping the body in balance.

12.7 Weight-Loss

Like diabetes, obesity has become a huge problem nowadays. The sedentary lifestyle we lead has caused people to become overweight or obese. The fact that machinery and devices make our life easier comes at a cost, and we are damaging our health. Moreover, obesity causes other diseases like type 1 diabetes, hypertension, and arthritis, which is caused by extra weight and pressure on the bones. Yoga provides a solution to all these problems. The best thing about it is that you do not have to practice demanding routines and diets in order to achieve the perfect body; yoga takes the whole body together and works at its own pace.

It takes more time, but you get better results. Another good thing about yoga is that it can be practiced at any age and provides solutions to problems of all kinds.

You can do basic exercises or most difficult ones, depending on your own requirements and needs.

Being overweight or obese makes many people feel depressed and not very confident.

But everyone is unique, and bodies come in all shapes and sizes. The "perfect body" is based on unrealistic standards, but living with an unhealthy body is also wrong.

Yoga may help you lose weight as well. It may take time, but in the end you will look fabulous because yoga also shapes your mind, creating the best version of yourself.

Chapter 13
Kundalini Meditations

This chapter is focused on how to practically implement kundalini meditations. You will find which meditations you can practice if you are a beginner. Remember that focus and consistency are the most important things to keep in mind, while practicing yoga.

The major goal is to reach a spiritual awakening, but you should always remember that there are no hard-and-fast rules. Everyone can experience it differently, or not experience it at all. Keep in mind that your journey is unique; comparing it with other people's journeys will only distract you from your focus.

When meditating, the main goal is to remove all the negative energy from your mind, heart, and soul and get rid of the emotional baggage we carry throughout our everyday life, which has an extremely negative effect on our body and mind. Always remember that kundalini yoga triggers your conscious and subconscious mind simultaneously.

Go into these meditations with a positive mind and slowly incorporate them in your daily routine. Before starting any meditation, you should always follow these steps:

- Choose a clean and calm place for meditation and practice it in the same place every day. This will help you focus energy and train your mind to associate this place with calm and peace.
- You should always wear something loose, comfortable, and made of natural fabrics so that you don't focus on your clothes being too tight or feeling rough on your skin.

- If possible, you should practice yoga in nature. Sounds like bird chirping, soft wind blowing, and the smell of grass can elevate the entire process.

Below you can find a few easy and beginner-friendly meditations.

13.1 The Prayer Pose

This is a really important pose in kundalini yoga meditations. We know that each body is a combination of positive and negative energy, and an electromagnetic charge runs throughout it. Now let's associate each side of the body with positive and negative energy.

The right side of the body represents positive energy, and the elements associated with it are the sun and masculine power. On the other hand, the left side of the body is associated with a negative charge or a negative electromagnetic field; the elements associated with it are the moon and feminine power. The masculine energy is known as the Pingala, while the feminine one is called Ida.

During the day, the frequency of both positive and negative energy is vastly fluctuating, which creates a disbalance in the state of calm and peace. By practicing the prayer pose, you can neutralize both energies and meditate peacefully. Remember that the human body is created as a neutral entity with an equal amount of positive and negative energy, and it works best when they are in sync. In this sense, the prayer pose helps you feel at peace.

Recommended Time

There is no hard and fast rules when it comes to how long you should perform this pose. Since it is easy and does not require a lot of effort, you can practice it at any time of the day. However, you will probably benefit more from it if you incorporate it to your morning routine.

Target Areas

The main target area is the mind, but this pose also affects the whole body. By practicing this pose, you neutralize positive and negative energies that flow through your body to meditate peacefully.

Frequency

You can practice meditation at any time of the day. However, it is recommended to start your day with this pose and a short meditation. It can be practiced up to five times a day, and frequency depends on your preferences and needs. Each one is different; some people only need to center their energies once a day, while others need to feel reenergized several times a day. In this sense, there are no hard and fast rules when it comes to kundalini yoga. Just listen to your body and choose you own routine.

Duration

The time duration for this specific position and meditation is around one to two minutes, and it can be repeated several times a day. However, you can practice it for up to five minutes according to your preference.

Pose

Choose a quiet corner to practice this pose. Whenever you practice kundalini yoga, you should be in nature. However, it is not compulsory at all.

Push both your hands against each other in a namaste pose so that the fingers are aligned. Now bring your hands up to your chest and touch the sternum with the back of your thumbs so that you feel a little pressure on the bone. Close your eyes and focus on center of your forehead, which is where the third eye is located.

The third eye symbolized infinite energy and consciousness beyond the world and is one of the main target points directed towards kundalini awakening.

During this pose, your thumbs apply pressure to the sternum; it triggers the vagus nerve, which is associated with all kinds of feelings and emotions.

Now, this pressure sends signals through the nerve and activates the pituitary gland in the brain. Therefore, hormones are secreted and create peace, neutralizing the energies that flow throughout the body.

Instructions

While holding the pose, keep your body stretched and relaxed. With your eyes closed, focus on the center of the forehead and breathe in and out at a normal pace. Keep inhaling and exhaling 25 to 30 times.

Mantra

There is no specific mantra for this meditation.

Conclusion

Meditate for 2 to 3 minutes, then open your palms and put your hands down on both sides of your body. Gradually open your eyes, take a deep breath, and slowly exhale. Repeat this deep breathing 5 times. It is believed that if you practice this meditation every day for about 30 days, you will be able to get rid of anxiety.

Recovery

Many people forget the importance of the recovery phase after meditation. The kundalini practice is centered around full circle and completeness. Now, when we do not bring our bodies to a proper conclusion of the meditation, we do not complete the full circle and cannot fully benefit from it. Remember that whenever you practice a specific meditation, bringing it to a proper conclusion is really important.

To recover from this prayer meditation, lay down on the floor with your legs slightly apart and your palms down on the side of your body. Close your eyes and inhale deeply to fill your lungs. Exhale lightly and repeat three to four times. Then get up and get started with your day.

13.2 Easy Breathing

This is the most basic type of kundalini yoga meditation and is suitable for beginners. As you already know, it is always recommended to start with easy meditations and then to increase the level.

However, you should always remember that even the most basic meditations can be practiced even if you are a yoga expert.

Recommended Time

Time is crucial when practicing meditation, but there are no hard and fast rules when it comes to it. However, it is recommended to practice this specific meditation between 2 pm and 4 pm.

Target Areas

This exercise is recommended when you feel physically and emotionally vulnerable and drained. Nowadays, our lives move faster than before; as a result, we don't have enough time to rest. Therefore, this meditation is very useful because it is easy to practice, helps regulate the body processes, and clears the mind.

Frequency

This meditation can be practiced up to three times a day. You can stick to once a day, but if you think you need to switch off and energize more, you can meditate up to three times a day.

Duration

This meditation is short and lasts about 3 to 5 minutes, while the recovery phase is 2 to 6 minutes.

It would help if you considered this breathing exercise like a warm-up. It recharges and regenerates your body but also acts as a transition to a state of calmness.

Pose

During any kind of meditation, sit comfortably, activate your mind, and make sure not to fall asleep.

Choose a quiet place and unroll your yoga mat. It is not compulsory to have one, but it really helps beginners with meditation.

Similarly, wearing specific clothes stimulates virtual association, preparing you for meditation.

To practice this meditation, sit with your legs crossed and stretch your back. Then join your palms in front of your chest and push them lightly against each other as if you were performing a namaste pose.

Instructions

This is a breathing exercise and helps your heart and mind. This meditation is mostly recommended to those seeking a clear mind and energy to manage daily tasks. If you suffer from mild anxiety and restlessness, you might benefit from this exercise. While sitting with your back straight, close your eyes and imagine yourself in a state of calm. Then inhale air in four steps, pulling your belly button inwards and filling your lungs should. Hold this position for 3 to 4 seconds and then exhale the same way, emptying your lungs. Then repeat this exercise two more times.

Mantra

In the previous chapter, we discussed and explained that kundalini yoga also involves spirituality. Therefore, each kundalini meditation incorporates a specific chant or mantra. Each mantra has a specific meaning and is believed to bring its own energy; repeating it enhances its effect on the body and may trigger spiritual peace and an awakening.

For this specific meditation, the chant is SA TA NA MA. Each syllable represents a step of human life. SA means "complete, full circle" and represents infinity. According to yogic beliefs, the human body is energy and cannot be destroyed. This means that human life changes its form but is never actually destroyed. The syllable SA represents thought and belief. The next syllable TA represents life as we see it. The syllable NA represents being dead, leaving this body and world. The syllable MA represents a new beginning and rebirth; the new shape the body takes after death is represented by this last syllable.

While inhaling, you can repeat this mantra along the four steps. Since it is a breathing meditation, you don't want to say the words out loud. Just repeat them in your mind and do the same, while exhaling.

Repeat the whole breathing exercise for three to five minutes. It is recommended to start with a three-minute meditation and gradually take up to five minutes.

You should meditate two to three times a day, but you can start by doing it once and then move upwards.

Conclusion

Since the breathing meditation and the mantra create energy within the body, you will need to properly release it and make sure that you won't be overwhelmed. To conclude this meditation, hold your position and press both your palms against each other, while inhaling. You will feel some pressure on your hands and wrists. Now hold your breath for five to eight seconds and then release without moving your hands.

Recovery

Since this meditation is easy, you might think you don't need to recover after it. However, it gives you a lot of energy, which you have to manage. Therefore, it's very important to recover after practicing it. All you have to do is laying down with your eyes closed, while inhaling and exhaling slowly for two to five minutes.

Summary

STEP 1

Sit down on the yoga mat, cross your legs, and join your palms in front of your chest. Close your eyes and make sure to that your body is completely relaxed.

STEP 2

Inhale, while pulling your belly button inwards and filling up your lungs in four steps. Do not exhale meanwhile.

STEP 3

Exhale through both nostrils in four steps and empty your lungs during part four. Remember not to inhale during this process, and repeat it 3 to 4 times.

STEP 4

Introduce the mantra SA TA NA MA. Chant this mantra silently both by inhaling and exhaling. Concentrate on the meditation and block out everything else. Repeat the breathing meditation for up to 3 minutes. You can increase the duration up to 5 minutes when you're used to it.

STEP 5

After finishing, hold the position and press your palms against each other. Now inhale and fill up your lungs with one long and deep breath. Hold the breath for 6 to 8 seconds. Now release the pressure on your hands without moving them apart and exhale deeply.

STEP 6

Relax your body by lying down on your back with your eyes closed. Breathe deeply for 2 to 5 minutes and get up slowly.

13.3 How to Bring Coordination to Your Body

This is another simple and effective meditation, whose main benefit is body coordination. It will adjust the body's rhythm and prepare it for kundalini yoga, while gaining calm and peace. This meditation can be practiced on its own or combined with other meditations.

It is also considered a warm-up meditation and is a good start for your yoga practice. As a matter of fact, it helps relax the body and clear the mind, which may also trigger a kundalini awakening.

Recommended Time

You can practice this meditation at any time of the day, but it's recommended to do it in the early morning.

Target Areas

The target areas are the heart and the throat chakra. This meditation is good for stress relief and emotional balance.

Sometimes our mind and our heart are not in sync; your mind is convinced about something, while emotions tell you otherwise. If you are in such a situation, this meditation is very helpful. Practice it every week to keep your emotional and mental health in check.

Frequency

Usually, it can be practiced two to three times a day, but the frequency can be increased or decreased according to your own needs.

Duration

At the beginning, this meditation should be practiced for 3 minutes, but with practice, you can increase its duration up to 11 minutes.

Pose

Sit down and lock your arms over your chest, tucking your hands under your armpits.

- Instruction:

First drink a glass of water because hydration helps keeping your emotions in balance. Then sit comfortably on the mat with your legs crossed.

After that, cross your arms around your chest and tuck your hands under the armpits. Now pull your shoulders towards the ear lobes, straighten your back, and bend your backbone backward, while bringing your jaw upwards.

Close your eyes and hold the position for 3 minutes, while breathing slowly. You should breathe four times per minute.

Mantra

This is silent meditation, so there's no specific mantra that we recommend.

Conclusion

Open your eyes, stretch out your arms and legs, and take five deep breaths.

Recovery

There is no recovery phase required for this meditation; however, if you want to relax your body, you can always lay down on your back and practice deep breathing for one or two minutes.

Summary

STEP 1

Drink a glass of water to keep your emotions in balance.

STEP 2

Sit comfortably on the mat with your legs crossed.

STEP 3

Cross your arms around your chest and tuck your hands under your armpits, and your palms must be straight.

STEP 4

Pull your shoulders towards the ear lobes, straighten your back, and bend your backbone backwards.

STEP 5

Close your eyes and hold this position for 3 minutes, while breathing slowly.

STEP 6

Open your eyes, stretch out your arms and legs, and take five deep breaths.

13.4 Meditation for Concentration

Recommended Time

The recommended time for this meditation is late evening or early morning.

Target Areas

The target areas are the mind and the third eye chakra. This meditation helps the mind being focused, while meditating.

Frequency

It can be practiced every day and two times a day in the morning and the evening.

Duration

It takes around three minutes.

Pose

Find your way to the rock pose by sitting comfortably on your heels.

Instructions

Raise your arms and on the top of your head and join your hands in the prayer position. Stretch your elbows and close your eyes so that only 1/10th of them is open. Press your arms against your ears, hold this position, and inhale. Hold your breath for 20 seconds and then fully exhale. Repeat it for three minutes.

Mantra

The mantra OM NAMO is optional. You don't want to say it out loud; repeat it in your head.

Conclusion

Open your eyes, stretch out your arms and legs, and take five deep breaths.

Recovery

There is no recovery phase required for this meditation; however, if you want to relax your body, you can always lay down on your back and practice deep breathing for one or two minutes.

Summary

Step 1

Raise your arms and on the top of your head and join your hands in the prayer position.

Step 2

Stretch your elbows.

Step 3

Close your eyes so that only 1/10th them is open.

Step 4

Press your arms against your ears, hold this position and inhale. Hold your breath for 20 seconds and then fully exhale. Repeat it three minutes.

Step 5

Open your eyes, stretch out your arms and legs, and take five deep breaths.

Step 6

There is no recovery phase required for this meditation; however, if you want to relax your body, you can always lay down on your back and practice deep breathing for one or two minutes.

13.5 Mahan Jaap

This is an intermediate group meditation. While practicing it, you will respond to other people's energy and to the environment around you.

Recommended Time

You must practice this meditation with together with other people and a guru, guiding you.

Target Areas

The target area is the third eye chakra, which helps with toning and nourishing mind and concentration.

The third eye chakra represents the connection between the spiritual and the physical world. Working on this chakra means improving your mental abilities as a human being.

Frequency

It can be practiced once a month since a group activity is always difficult to arrange.

Duration

For a large group, the duration can be around 11 to 30 minutes.

Pose

The pose is the sat kriya, where your arms are placed on your knees.

Instructions

Sit along with other group members in a room. Close your eyes and concentrate on the third eye point, while starting to chant the mantra SA TA NA MA out loud. Now every member takes it in turns to chant the mantra. Continue for at least 11 minutes and then you open your eyes.

Mantra

SA TA NA MA.

Conclusion

Inhale and exhale for two minutes.

Recovery

There is no specified recovery for this meditation.

Summary

STEP 1

All group members are sitting in a room.

STEP 2

They close their eyes and concentrate on the third eye point.

STEP 3

With ultimate concentration, the guru starts chanting the mantra SA TA NA MA.

STEP 4

Then everyone takes it in turns to say it out loud.

STEP 5

They continue like this for at least 11 minutes and then open their eyes.

13.6 Breathing Through Alternate Nostrils

This is one of the most famous meditations all around the world. It helps keep in balance and activate both brain hemispheres. You can practice meditation by breathing through alternate nostrils or exclusively through one nostril. However, breathing through one particular nostril has specific effects on your body.

Breathing through the right nostril is beneficial for:

- Willpower
- Action
- Alertness
- Vigor

Breathing through the left nostril is beneficial for:

- Sensitivity
- Empathy
- Calmness
- Clearing the mind

Recommended Time

You should practice it in the morning, and preferably in nature.

Target Areas

The target areas are both sides of the brain, which are provided with balance. Most of the time we only use the left side of the brain, causing the right one to be under stimulated. By practicing this meditation, you can activate it as well.

Frequency

Breathing meditations can be performed up to three times a week. If you wish, you can do them every day as well.

Duration

There are no hard and fast rules associated with breathing meditations. But a good start can be 3 minutes for each nostril.

Pose

The pose is the sat kriya.

Procedure

There are two different breathing methods. The first one consists in breathing alternately through both nostrils, while the second one is breathing exclusively through one nostril.

If you chose the second method, sit down, relax, and perform a neck lock. Close your eyes and use your thumb to close one nostril. Now breath exclusively from the open nostril, take deep breaths, and empty your lungs when exhaling.

If you chose the first method, use your index finger and thumb to close one side of your nose. Then inhale from the other side. Now hold your breath, and then close this nostril with the index finger. Open the nostril you had closed with the thumb and exhale fully. Repeat this for up to three minutes.

Mantra

No mantra is chanted during this meditation.

Conclusion

Since this is a relaxing meditation itself, there is no specific conclusion for this meditation.

Recovery

There is no need to recover from this meditation because it is relaxing itself.

Summary

Breathing through one nostril:

STEP 1

Sit down and relax.

STEP 2

Perform a neck lock, close your eyes, and use your thumb to close one nostril.

STEP 3

Now breath exclusively from the open nostril, take deep breaths, and empty your lungs when exhaling.

Breathing through alternating nostrils:

STEP 1

Use your index finger and thumb to close one side of your nose and inhale from the other side.

STEP 2

Hold your breath and close this nostril with the index finger.

STEP 3

Now open the nostril you had closed with the thumb and exhale fully. Repeat it for up to three minutes.

13.7 Salabhasana Meditation

This asana is also known as the locust posture and treats intestinal diseases and infertility. However, it also tones thighs and shins and helps with insomnia. If you perform it daily, you will be able to sleep well every night.

Recommended Time

The recommended time to practice this meditation is in the early evening.

Target Areas

The target areas are the small intestine and legs. This meditation strengthens the flexibility of all skeletal muscles and bones, but it also has a positive effect on your overall well- being. If you incorporate it into your regular yoga routine, you will feel like you've changed and become more open to new ideas.

Frequency

It can be performed once a day or more often if required.

Duration

It takes around 4 to 5 minutes to perform this meditation.

Pose

The pose a relaxed lying down pose with one hand on the chin.

Instructions

Lay down on the yoga mat, place your right hand on your chin, and place the other hand beside your torso. Now raise your left leg as high as you can without bending it. Hold it for 10 seconds and slowly bring the leg down. Repeat it 5 to 6 times. Then place your left hand on your chin and repeat the same procedure with the other leg.

Mantra

The mantra LAM can be chanted when you move your leg upwards.

Conclusion

Lay down and practice one minute of deep breathing.

Summary

Step 1

Lay down straight on the yoga mat.

Step 2

Place your right hand on your chin.

Step 3

Place the other hand beside your torso.

Step 4

Raise your left leg as high as you can without bending it.

Step 5

Hold it for 10 seconds and slowly bring the leg down.

Step 6

Repeat it 5 to 6 times. Then place your left hand on your chin and repeat the same procedure with the other leg.

13.8 Trikonasana Meditation

This asana effectively treats uterine diseases, but it cannot be performed during your period. It tones hips, thighs, legs, and the tummy and is also helpful for skin, bladder, and kidneys.

Recommended Time

The recommended time of the day is in the mid-afternoon.

Target Areas

The target areas are the root chakra and the sacral chakra. The root chakra is associated with sexual health, while the sacral chakra is associated with the digestive system. Moreover, both of them play a big role in getting rid of toxins and improving mental health. Since this asana is so beneficial, you should incorporate it to your yoga routine and perform it at least once a day.

Frequency

This can be performed from one to three times a day.

Duration

The meditation takes around 5 to 6 minutes.

Pose

The pose is a simple lying-down pose.

Instructions

Lay down on the floor with one arm under your head and the other spread out. Keep both your legs straight together and then slowly lift one of them. Make sure that your toes are pointing upwards. Hold this position for 10 seconds and then bring your leg down. Now do the same with the other leg and repeat for three minutes, while alternating your legs.

Mantra

There is no specific mantra for this meditation.

Conclusion

Lay down with your arms on both sides of your torso and your legs slightly apart. Practice deep breathing for one minute.

Recovery

Breathe deeply and drink a glass of water at room temperature.

Summary

Step 1

Lay down on the floor with one arm under your head and the other spread out.

Step 2

Keep both your legs straight together.

Step 3

Lift one leg and make sure that your toes are pointing upwards.

Step 4

Hold this position for 10 seconds and bring your leg down. Then do the same exercise with the other leg and repeat it for three minutes, while alternating your legs.

13.9 Savasana Meditation

While practicing this posture, your body is relaxing. Savasana meditation tones your muscles and improves your mental and respiratory functions. It is as simple and easy as taking a nap after lunch; as a result, you will feel lighter.

***Recommended Time** In the midafternoon.*

Target Areas

The target areas are the mind and respiratory system. This meditation is directed towards the third eye chakra and the heart chakra.

The third eye chakra regulates the mind and keeps your thoughts in check. Similarly, the heart chakra regulates the respiratory system and provides tone to lungs and other respiratory organs.

Frequency

Once or twice a day, depending on your needs.

Duration

Around 10 minutes.

Pose

Savasana.

Instructions

Lay down on the floor with your legs slightly open. Then stretch both your arms and get loose, trying to consciously get rid of stress.

Do not stretch your muscles too much and keep your chin relaxed. Now close your eyes and take a deep breath with your mouth open.

Mantra

The mantra chanted during this meditation is LAAM.

Conclusion

Since this is a relaxing meditation, there is no conclusion required.

Recovery

Since this is a relaxing meditation, there is no recovery required.

Summary

STEP 1

Lay down on the floor with your legs slightly open. Then stretch your arms and get loose.

STEP 2

Lie down comfortably and try to consciously get rid of stress. Do not stretch your muscles too much.

STEP 3

Keep your chin relaxed, close your eyes, and take a deep breath with your mouth open.

13.10 Three-Stroke Breathing Meditation

The three-stroke breathing meditation is very simple and suitable for beginners. It helps open up heart, throat, and mind.

Recommended Time

It can be practiced at any time of the day.

Target Areas

The target areas are the heart and the throat chakra, which are connected to each other. The heart chakra is associated with feelings, while the throat chakra is responsible for expressing your feelings with confidence.

By practicing this meditation, you can unblock the energy flow through the heart and throat chakra.

Frequency

It can be practiced every day or once a week.

Duration

Around 15 minutes.

Pose

The head must be in the neck lock position.

Instructions

Sit down with your legs crossed. Join your hands in front of your chest, but do not interlace the fingers. Close your eyes and breathe from the mouth in three strokes, while pressing with your hands.

Now exhale in one stroke with your nose and continue for about 15 minutes.

Mantra

This is a breathing exercise, so no mantra is required.

Conclusion

Perform deep breathing for one minute to conclude the meditation.

Recovery

This is an intense breathing exercise. After this meditation, you should have a glass of warm water or green tea.

Summary

STEP 1

Sit down with your legs crossed.

STEP 2

Join your hands in front of your chest, but do not interlace the fingers.

STEP 3

Close your eyes and breathe from your mouth in three strokes, while pressing with your hands at each stroke. Now exhale in one stroke with your nose.

STEP 4

Continue for about 15 minutes.

13.11 Meditation for Happiness

The main focus of yoga is to find happiness, and this meditation helps with it. Most of the time, we do not realize that the happiness we have been searching for is within us, and we were looking for it elsewhere.

Recommended Time

Early in the morning before dawn.

Target Areas

This meditation is related to feelings and openness and is targeted at the heart and third eye chakra. The heart chakra opens up your heart, making you experience love and empathy. As a result, your body radiates positive energy and is open to absorbing even more positivity from your surroundings. When you radiate positive vibes, you create a positive aura around your body, attracting positive energy as well.

Frequency

This meditation can be performed more than once a day. However, even practicing it just once a day for a month will be beneficial. This is recommended for people who are feeling sad and unhappy.

Duration

Around five minutes.

Pose

Stretch your back and perform a Jalandhar bandh.

Procedure

Sit down in a calm and quiet place with your head in the neck lock. Place your hands on your knees and relax them. Now close your eyes and focus on the third eye. Chant ONG for 10 seconds through your nose and not through your mouth. Meanwhile, keep your mouth slightly open and breathe through your nose. Repeat it five times and gradually reduce the chanting to 5 seconds.

Mantra

The mantra used in this meditation is ONG.

Conclusion

The conclusion of this meditation is deep breathing for one minute.

Recovery

This meditation is not very intense, so the recovery phase will not be necessary.

Summary

STEP 1

Sit down in a calm and quiet place with your head in the neck lock.

STEP 2

Place your hands on your knees and relax them.

STEP 3

Close your eyes and focus on the third eye. Now chant ONG for 10 seconds through your nose and not through your mouth.

STEP 4

Keep your mouth should slightly open and breathe from the nose.

STEP 5

Repeat five times and then reduce the chanting to 5 seconds.

13.12 Meditation to Face Tomorrow

Now and then, you may face difficult times and challenges. This meditation is good for such times because it improves your confidence and wisdom.

Recommended Time

Late evening or nighttime.

Target Areas

The target areas are the throat chakra and the heart chakra. This meditation is good for people with low self-esteem and lack of confidence. In this sense, performing this meditation before a big meeting or a presentation can help you a lot because it unblocks your voice and thoughts, while reducing anxiety and providing you with a sense of calm and security.

Frequency

Once a day or once a week.

Duration

Around 10 minutes.

Pose

Neck lock.

Instructions

This meditation consists of three parts. First, sit and close your eyes, while focusing on your chin. Now lift your arms to your shoulder and then keep your hands with your palms down. Hold this position for three minutes and keep breathing naturally.

Next, turn your hands with your arms upwards. While breathing normally, hold this position for three minutes.

Now, turn your hands outwards with the pinky finger in the upper position and the thumb in the lower position. Hold this position for then minutes.

Mantra

None.

Conclusion

With your hands on your lap, practice deep breathing for one minute.

Recovery

None.

Summary

STEP 1

Sit down and close your eyes, while focusing on your chin.

STEP 2

Now lift your arms to your shoulder and keep your hands with palms down.

STEP 3

Hold this position for three minutes and keep breathing naturally. Then turn your hands with your arms upwards and hold the position for three minutes.

Step 4

Turn your hands outwards with the pinky finger in the upper position and the thumb in the lower position. Hold this position for three minutes.

13.13 Meditation for a Better Future

Everyone wants a better and brighter future. You can practice this meditation when you have a specific goal for your future and want to achieve it at all costs. It's a three-step meditation that takes around 15 to 20 minutes.

Recommended Time

This is an intermediate meditation, and you should practice it on an empty stomach early in the afternoon.

Target Areas

The target areas are the heart chakra and the third eye chakra. Focusing on the heart chakra has positive effects both on your body and on your mind. If energy flows freely through this chakra, the pituitary gland is activated, regulating the secretion of hormones, and helping you control your emotions.

Frequency

Once a week or once a month.

Duration

Around 15 to 20 minutes.

Pose

Sit down and perform a Gyan mudra. Keep your back straight and your chest forward. Then close your eyes and place your arms on your knees.

Instructions

This meditation consists in three parts. First, sit down, keep your back straight and your chest forward. Put your arms on your knees and perform the Gyan mudra. Now close your eyes and focus on the third eye area.

Now inhale through your mouth and keep it open in a rounded shape. Then close it and exhale through the nostrils. Repeat this process for 5 to 7 minutes.

After five minutes, inhale normally and hold your breath. Meanwhile, meditate focusing on the term "zero" (e.g., "I am zero, the world is zero, and everything around me is zero"). Then exhale and inhale again.

Continue for 5 to 7 minutes. Then focus on your main goal for your future. Go on breathing and concentrate on your wish, while holding your breath. Continue for 7 minutes and then relax.

Mantra

None.

Conclusion

This is an intense meditation, so you must stretch your arms and your legs breathe deeply for 2 minutes afterwards.

Recovery

You can lay down in the corpse pose and practice deep breathing for 2 minutes.

Summary

Step 1

This meditation consists in three parts. First, sit down and keep your back straight and your chest forward.

Step 2

Put your arms on your knees and perform the Gyan mudra. Now close your eyes and focus on the third eye area.

Step 3

Inhale through your mouth and keep it open in a rounded shape.

Step 4

Now close your mouth and exhale slowly through the nostrils.

Step 5

Repeat this process for 5 to 7 minutes. After five minutes, inhale normally and hold your breath. Focus on the term "zero", while holding your breath. Then exhale and continue for 5 to 7 minutes.

Step 6

Now focus on your main goal for the future. Go on breathing for 7 minutes.

STEP 7

After the meditation, stretch your arms and your legs and breathe deeply for 2 minutes.

STEP 8

Lay down in the corpse pose and practice deep breathing for 2 minutes.

13.14 Kirtan Kriya

This advanced meditation is focused on the third eye and the crown chakra and helps achieve knowledge and wisdom. If you practice it for two and a half hours every day for one year, you will see the results, and you may also trigger a kundalini awakening.

Recommended Time

Preferably, early in the morning, or when you can fully concentrate without being disturbed.

- Targeted Areas:

The targeted areas are the third eye chakra and the crown chakra. The third eye is believed to be placed in the center of the forehead; however, its actual location is in the central brain and near the pituitary gland. These two chakras are associated with the highest level of consciousness and self-awareness. As a matter of fact, most of the meditations that focus on these chakras help you become a better version of yourself.

Frequency

Once a week. However, you can practice it every day if your main goal is to trigger a kundalini awakening.

Duration

11 to 31 minutes.

Pose

Sit down, form a Jalandhar bandh, keep your back straight, and push your chest forward. At the beginning, perform the Gyan mudra; then alternate it with Shuni mudra, Surya mudra, and Buddhi mudra.

Instructions

Sit down with your neck straight and stretch out your chest. Close your eyes and then concentrate on the third eye.

Chant the mantra is SA TA NA MA and perform Gyan, Shuni, Surya, and Buddhi mudra alternately. Associate SA with the Gyan mudra, TA with the Shuni mudra, NA with the Surya mudra, and MA with the Buddhi mudra. Continue chanting aloud for 5 minutes.

Then whisper your mantra for another five minutes. After that, keep quiet and chant it in your mind for five more minutes. Now change the process and start chanting silently for ten minutes. Then whisper your mantra five minutes and say it aloud for another five minutes. Finish your meditation by laying down in a corpse pose and practicing deep breathing for five minutes. Since this is an intense meditation, you should drink some water afterwards.

Mantra

SA TA NA MA.

Conclusion

Lay down in a corpse pose and deep breathing for 5 minutes.

Recovery

Drink a glass of water at room temperature.

Summary

STEP 1

Sit down with your neck straight and stretch out your chest. Close your eyes and then concentrate on the third eye.

STEP 2

Chant the mantra is SA TA NA MA and perform Gyan, Shuni, Surya and Buddhi mudra alternately. Associate SA with the Gyan mudra, TA with the Shuni mudra, NA with the Surya mudra, and MA with the Buddhi mudra. Continue chanting aloud for 5 minutes.

STEP 3

Then whisper your mantra for five minutes. After that, keep quiet and chant it in your mind for five minutes. Now change the process and start chanting silently for ten minutes.

STEP 4

Then whisper your mantra for five minutes and say it aloud for other five minutes.

STEP 5

Finish your meditation by laying down in a corpse pose and practicing deep breathing for five minutes.

STEP 6

Drink a glass of water at room temperature.

13.15 Calm Heart Meditation

This meditation is targeted towards the heart chakra, provides tone to the heart muscle, and regulates blood circulation. It also improves your mood, making you feel safe and less anxious.

- Recommended time:

Any time of the day.

Target Areas

The target area is the heart chakra. By practicing this meditation, you will become more open, accepting, and empathetic.

Practicing meditations that are directed to the throat charka also has a positive effect on the heart and the circulatory system.

Frequency

Once or twice a day.

Duration

At least three minutes.

Pose

Just sit down and perform the Gyan mudra.

Instructions

Sit down and close your eyes with your head in Jalandhar bandh. Focus on the heart chakra and place your left hand on your heart with palms on your chest and fingers parallel to the ground. Now raise the right hand as if you were taking an oath. Now touch the tip of the thumb with the tip of the index finger, while keeping the other fingers straight. Hold this position for three minutes and then relax.

Mantra

None.

Conclusion

None.

Recovery

None.

Summary

Step 1

Sit down and close your eyes with your head in Jalandhar bandh.

Step 2

Focus on the heart chakra.

Step 3

Place your left hand on your heart with the palms on your chest and the fingers parallel to the ground.

Step 4

Raise your right hand as if you were taking an oath. Now touch the tip of the thumb with the tip of the index finger, while keeping the other fingers straight.

Step 5

Hold this position for three minutes and then relax.

13.16 Meditation for Wisdom

Everyone wants to be wise, but what is wisdom? To be wise means to reflect on yourself, to not go with the flow, to create principles, to talk with clarity, and to be just in your dealings.

Even if the path to wisdom is not easy, this meditation can help you.

Recommended Time

Early in the morning.

Target Areas

Sacral chakra.

Frequency

Once a week or once a month.

Duration

31 minutes.

Pose

Sitting pose.

Procedure

Sit down and close your eyes. Then raise your hands and bend your elbows. Your hands should be in a cup shape and held in front of you. Focus on the tip of your nose.

Now start squeezing your navel until you can easily do it. After 10 seconds, exhale and then start squeezing again. Repeat this for thirty minutes.

Mantra

None.

Conclusion

This is quite an intense meditation. After finishing, stretch your arms and legs and then practice deep breathing for 5 minutes.

Recovery Phase:

Lay down in the cobra pose and practice deep breathing for three minutes. Try not to fall asleep.

Summary

Step 1

Sit down and close your eyes.

Step 2

Raise your hands and bend your elbows. Your hands should be in a cupping shape and held in front of you.

Step 3

Focus on the tip of your nose. Then start squeezing your navel until you can easily do it. After 10 seconds, exhale.

Step 4

Start squeezing it again. Repeat this for thirty minutes.

Step 5

After meditation, stretch your arms and legs and then practice deep breathing for 5 minutes.

STEP 6

Lay down in the cobra pose and then practice deep breathing for three minutes. Try not to fall sleep.

13.17 Meditation to Overcome Self Animosity

Sometimes we are our own enemies. However, this meditation can help you accept yourself and get rid of self-destructive behaviors.

Recommended Time

Early in the morning or late afternoon.

Target Areas

The heart and the throat chakra.

Frequency

Every day, but up to 22 minutes.

Duration

3 minutes (beginner)-22 minutes (advanced).

Pose

Sitting pose.

Instructions

Sit down with your head in the neck lock. Stretch your back and open your chest. Now close your eyes and focus on the tip of the nose. Raise your hands in front of the chest and form two fists. Now release both thumbs and point them upwards, while pressing the fists against each other. Breathe deeply through the mouth and exhale through the nose. Then inhale through the nose and exhale through the mouth. Alternate mouth and nose breathing for 3 to 11 minutes.

Mantra

None.

Conclusion

None.

Recovery

None.

Summary

Step 1

Sit down with your head in a neck lock.

Step 2

Stretch your back and open your chest. Close your eyes and focus on the tip of the nose.

Step 3

Raise your hands in front of your chest and form two fists.

Step 4

Now release both thumbs and point them upwards, while pressing the fists against each other. Breathe deeply through the mouth and exhale through the nose. Then inhale through the nose and exhale through the mouth.

STEP 5

Alternate mouth and nose breathing

for 3 to 11 minutes.

13.18 Meditation to Increase Spiritual Stamina

This is a strengthening meditation. Sometimes you can feel emotionally drained; therefore, you should always try to reenergize your body and build your spiritual stamina.

Recommended Time

Early in the morning, when the cosmic energies are at their peak.

Target Areas

The third chakra.

Instructions

Sit down, close your eyes, and focus on the third eye chakra. Perform a Jalandhar bandh, raise your hands above your head, and join your fingers. Breathe normally and hold this position for three minutes.

Frequency

Once a week.

Duration

3 minutes to 11 minutes.

Pose

Sitting pose and Venus lock mudra.

Mantra

None.

Conclusion

Practice deep breathing for two minutes after finishing the exercise.

Recovery

None.

Summary

STEP 1

Sit down.

STEP 2

Close your eyes, focus on the third eye chakra, and perform a Jalandhar bandh. Raise your hands above your head and join your fingers.

STEP 3

Breathe normally and hold this position for three minutes.

STEP 4

Practice deep breathing for two minutes after finishing the exercise.

STEP 5

There is no need to recover after this meditation.

13.19 Seven Hours of Guided Meditation.

We have discussed 18 important meditations so far. Now you will find out more about another beginner-friendly meditation.

Usually, yoga is practiced for 30 to 40 minutes each day. However, you can sometimes do this 7-hour meditation. You start in the morning on an empty stomach so that no energy from your surroundings can influence you. Before the meditation, drink some water or tea and eat some fruit, which is the only type of food you will consume during the day. Even though the meditation lasts for seven hours, the cleansing process will take you 24 hours.

Below you can find some rules that you must follow, while practicing this meditation:

- You must wear white clothes, and maybe a turban or a scarf on your head so that you can block negative energies around your aura.
- You must choose a quiet location to practice without being disturbed.
- If possible, you must practice this meditation in nature.
- You must bring a water bottle and some fruit with you.
- You mustn't speak during the meditation, except for the chants.

Below you can find other recommendations regarding this meditation:

- Start meditating at 6 am on an empty stomach and only drink a glass of water.
- Start with the prayer pose:
    » Name: Prayer Pose

Duration 5 minutes

» Timing: 6 am to 6.10 am.

Instructions

The procedure is fairly simple. Once you got into the prayer pose, keep your body straight and relaxed. Now close your eyes and concentrate on the center of the forehead, while inhaling and exhaling at normal pace 25 to 30 times.

Target Areas

The main target area is the mind, but this meditation also affects the whole body.

- Drink a glass of water and relax.
- Now perform easy breathing.

    » Name: Easy Breathing

Duration 15 minutes

» Timing: 6.20 am to 6.35 am

Instructions

This is a breathing exercise that helps regulate the heart rate. It is mostly recommended to those seeking clarity of the mind and energy for day-to-day tasks. Moreover, if you suffer from mild anxiety and restlessness, you might benefit from this exercise.

Sit down or your mat while keeping your back straight and your palms together. Now close your eyes and imagine yourself in a state of calm. Inhale in four steps and pull your belly button inwards. When you inhale the last time, fill your lungs. completely. Hold this position for 3 to 4 seconds and exhale the same way in four steps, emptying your lungs completely. Repeat this process two more times for 15 minutes.

Target Areas

This exercise is recommended when you feel physically and emotionally vulnerable and drained. Compared to thirty years ago, our lives are much busier. Therefore, we often need to give ourselves some time to regain strength and energize our bodies. This meditation is useful because it's easy to practice, regulates the body systems, and clears your mind.

- Now relax for approximately 5 minutes.
- Next perform this meditation to increase the spiritual stamina.
  - » Name: Meditation to increase spiritual stamina.

Duration 22 minutes

  » Time: 6.40 am to 7.02 am

Instructions

First of all, sit down, close your eyes, and focus on the third eye chakra. Preform a Jalandhar bandh and raise your hands above your head, joining your fingers. Breath normally and hold this position for 3 minutes.

- Now drink a glass of water and take a break for half an hour. Just sit by yourself and go into deep thinking.
- After resting, start the meditation for wisdom.
  - » Name: Meditation for wisdom

Duration 31 minutes

  » Time: 7.30 am to 8.00 am

Instructions

Sit down and close your eyes. Then raise your hands and bend your elbows. Your hands should be in a cup shape and held in front of you. While keeping your eyes closed, focus on the tip of your nose, and start squeezing your navel. Now wait for 10 seconds, exhale, and start squeezing it again. Repeat the process for thirty minutes.

> » Target areas:

The target area is the sacral chakra, which is associated with stomach, intestines, and the kidneys.

- Now lay down on the floor and do the corpse pose for 10 minutes. During this pose, close your eyes and focus on the third eye chakra.
- Take half a glass of water and drink it in two steps.
- If you are with other people, sit together with them. If you are alone, you can skip this part.
- Now perform the Mahaan Jaap

> » Name: Mahaan Jaap

Duration 30 minutes

> » Time: 8:10 am to 8:40 am

Instructions

While sitting together with others, close your eyes and concentrate on the third eye. With ultimate concentration, start chanting the mantra SA TA NA MA. After the guru, every member takes turns to chant the mantra. Continue for at least 11 minutes and then you open your eyes.

- Now perform the Trikonasana Meditation

> » Name: Trikonasana

Duration 5 minutes

> » Time: 8.40am to 8.50am

Instructions

Lay down on the floor with one arm under your head and the other spread out. Keep both your legs straight together. Then slowly lift your leg and make sure that your toes are pointing upwards. Keep your leg in this position for 10 seconds and then bring it down. Now do the same with the other leg. Repeat, while alternating legs for 3 minutes.

Target Areas

The focus areas are the root and the sacral chakra. Therefore, this meditation helps your sexual health and your digestive system.

- Now take a one-hour break. During the break, you should have a warm cup of ginger tea and a full glass of water towards the end of the break.
- If you feel exhausted and sleepy, don't worry. It means that you have been doing the meditation correctly.
- Now do the alternate nostril meditation.
    - » Name: Alternate nostril meditation

Duration 6 minutes.

- » Time: 9.40 am to 9.50 am

Instructions

There is no hard and fast rule associated with breathing meditations. However, a good reference point can be 3 minutes for each nostril. After breathing in a quiet place, perform the sat kriya pose.

Instructions

There are two different breathing methods.

The first method is the alternate nostril breathing, while the other second one consists in breathing exclusively from one nostril. If you chose the second method, sit down with your head in a neck lock. Now close our eyes and use our thumb to close one nostril. Breath exclusively from the open nostril, take deep breaths, and empty the lungs when exhaling.

If you are practicing the alternate nostril breathing, use your index finger and thumb to close one side of your nose. Inhale from the other nostril and hold your breath. Now close this nostril with the index finger and open the other one. Exhale fully and repeat the process for up to three minutes.

> » Target areas:

The main target area is the mind, but this meditation also affects the whole body.

- Now practice a meditation to become more confident and be able to face challenges.
    > » Name: Facing tomorrow meditation.

Duration 30 mins

> » Time: 10 am to 10.30 am

Instructions

This meditation consists in three parts. First of all, sit down and close your eyes. Now focus on your chin, lift your arms, and then keep your hands with the palms down. Hold this position for 3 minutes and keep breathing naturally. Next, turn your hands and your arms upwards and keep this position for three minutes, while breathing naturally. Lastly, turn your hands outwards with the pinky finger in the upper position and the thumb in the lower position. Hold this position for 3 minutes and finish the meditation.

> » Target areas:

The target areas are the heart and throat chakra. This meditation helps people with low self-esteem who want to become more confident.

- After this practice the prayer pose for 30 minutes again. Focus on the third eye chakra in the center of your forehead.
- Now, take another one-hour break, walk around, and stretch your body. Take another cup of tea followed by a glass of water at room temperature. Remember to drink slowly.
- Now perform the kirtan kriya.

  » Name: Kirtan kriya

Duration 1 hour

  » Time: 12 pm to 1 pm

Instructions

Sit down with your neck straight and stretch your chest. Now close your eyes and concentrate on the third eye location. The mantra for this meditation is SA TA NA MA, while the mudras are Gyan, Shuni, Surya, and Buddhi mudras. Chant SA with Gyan mudra, TA with the Shuni mudra, NA with Surya mudra, and MA with Buddhi mudra. Chant out loud for 5 minutes; then whisper the mantra for another five minutes. After that, keep quiet and chant in your mind for five more minutes.

Now reverse the sequence and start with the silent chanting for 10 minutes. Now whisper for five minutes and chant out loud for five more minutes. Finish the meditation by laying down in a corpse pose and practicing deep breathing for 5 minutes. Since this is an intense meditation, drink water afterwards.

  » Target areas:

The targeted areas are the third eye and the crown chakra.

Conclusion

By the end of the book, you must have learnt a lot of things about yoga and be intrigued by the mystical journey of kundalini yoga. Yoga is an ancient discipline that has been practiced in Asia for a long time; however, it is fairly new to the Western world. The benefits of yoga have been kept secret for thousands of years because this knowledge and level of consciousness are believed to be sacred. This is why this knowledge had not become common among the Western world population before the 1960s. This was around the same time that the hippie movement was arising, and the young people were looking for spirituality, consciousness, and deep meaning of life. Yoga provided them a structured way, a disciplined routine, and an effective method towards divinity. After that, there was no looking back for yoga.

This book is focused on kundalini yoga and the attainment of spiritual awakening. This practice is especially relevant nowadays. We are working more than ever, earning more than ever, but all that wealth cannot buy us happiness and peace. Something is missing, that is recognizing the purpose of life. Kundalini yoga guides you to reach your maximum potential as a human being, remove the blocks in your energy flow, and release the energy placed within your body.

Kundalini does not magically grant you energy and enables you to identify the energy within your body. It helps you clear the fogginess in your mind and gain consciousness; when the peak is reached, you may be able to experience kundalini awakening, which is different for everyone.

To understand the concept of Kundalini yoga, you must first understand what yoga is and where it originated. You must also focus on the main goal you are trying to achieve. If you don't take it seriously, you will only waste time and energy. Kundalini yoga is something that needs time, serious dedication, and consistency. If you are willing to invest this much, then only you can reap the full benefits of it. This book will guide you towards the right path to start your journey to peace and calm by explaining you the history of yoga, the different types of yoga, and the practice of kundalini yoga in detail.

The book focuses on the meaning, ideology, and process of kundalini yoga. Chakras are discussed in detail because these seven energy centers are the main components on which the entire process is based. We often read about chakras, and this word is casually thrown into conversations, but it's not always fully clear to us what it really means. Here you have learned in-depth about chakras and their benefits. As a result, you can associate the specific parts of the body and energy centers to the specific emotion and energy, which will help you flow through these chakras if you experience any block.

Meditations are also described in detail to make you really understand them. Moreover, at the end of each meditation, you are given a summary. Once you have understood them, you can quickly go through them and incorporate them in your daily routine.

Kundalini yoga has many benefits on health, especially on the nervous system. By bringing calm and peace to the mind, it stimulates the neurons and helps reduce stress and anxiety. Furthermore, the mind becomes stronger and is trained to remain neutral during stressful situations. It also has a positive effect on your willpower, and you become more focused, strong-willed, and resilient. You will feel this rush of energy through your body that you have never experienced before.

Practicing kundalini makes you physically stronger and much more flexible. Since the kundalini practice focuses on feminine energy, it regulates and enhances sexual desirability and ability. The lower part of the body, which is associated with the coiled snake, is where the reproductive organs are placed as well. Thus, this practice stimulates and enhances your sexual activity and helps you recognize your sexual power and ability. As a result, you feel more confident about your sexuality.

This book is for everyone; either you are a beginner or an expert, you will find something interesting in it. At the beginning, you will find a description of all types of yoga, its basics, and origins. After that, you will be provided a detailed account of kundalini yoga, its history, and terminology. In the end, you will find a comprehensive account of yoga meditations and guided techniques.

Last but not the least, kundalini yoga is an overall booster of health and wellbeing, and this aspect is explained plainly and in detail. This will encourage you to go deeper into the study and practice of kundalini yoga.

I am sure you will find a few minutes of your time to review my hard work! Thank you, and I send you love!

Made in the USA
Columbia, SC
22 December 2023